Richard Wolff

Richard Wolff was born in Germany, lived in Belgium for thirteen years, and came to the United States In 1951. He has written and broadcast for German, French and American audiences.

Wolff travels extensively on behalf of Living Letters Overseas, serves as a professional consultant and is president of the board of International Christian Broadcasters.

Among the works authored by Richard Wolff are several commentaries and books focusing on contemporary issues such as **Is God Dead?,** a critique of radical theologians, **Israel Act III,** an analysis of the current situation in Israel, **Riots In The Streets,** dealing with the problem of racial unrest and **Man at the Top,** a study of creative leadership.

THE MEANING
OF LONELINESS

THE MEANING
OF LONELINESS

by

RICHARD WOLFF

Key Publishers
Wheaton, Illinois 60187

Table of Contents

Introduction by Billy Graham   7

1. Loneliness   9

2. The Burden of Loneliness   15

3. The Causes of Loneliness   23
   Psychiatric Analysis   23
   Historic Perspectives   28
   Sociological Conjectures   31

4. The Cures of Loneliness   41

5. Levels of Loneliness   47
   Man Alone   48
   Man and Man   50
   Man and God   54

6. The Remedy   67

7. Loneliness of Godly Men   75

8. Solitude   91

9. Friendship   101

10. The Single Life   109

11. The Balance   121

12. Conclusion   129

INTRODUCTION

Richard Wolff has not only given us THE MEAN-ING OF LONELINESS — he has suggested many of its causes, and has given us the only specific cure for this modern syndrome of man.

Loneliness has plagued mankind through the centuries, and the author is right when he says that its chief cause is our alienation from God. In the opening words of Genesis God said, "It is not good that the man shall be alone." Loneliness can be caused on the horizontal plane by man's separation from man. But, it can be caused in the vertical sphere by man's separation from God. Gregarious man cannot fully live unto himself and know serenity and inner peace.

Richard Wolff in this volume has focused our attention on the problem of loneliness in a penetrating and stimulating manner. If you have been grappling with loneliness the truths outlined in this book should give you inspiration and help.

BILLY GRAHAM

1

LONELINESS

The funeral procession moved across the city till it reached the ancient city gate. A young man had died. His mother, a widow, had torn her garment in passionate grief. Sitting on the floor and refusing to eat or drink, she had mourned her only son. Finally the moment had come. The body was lifted on a bier and carried by friends and neighbors, anxious to share in the good deed. Hired flutists played their lamentations; shrill and melancholy sounds enveloped the funeral cortege. The widow wept. There was no courage, only emptiness.

At the city gate they met another crowd, following a stranger. Which crowd would give way to the other? The stranger said: Young man, I say to you, arise. The dead man sat up and began to speak. The prince of life had conquered. Jesus gave the young man back to his mother and she who had mourned as one mourns an only son was comforted. She was no longer alone.

— · —

Capernaum was a flourishing urban center. It was a landing place for boats crossing the lake and a key city on the road which linked Damascus with the Mediterranean ports. The tax office was a busy place, but Levi was a lonely man. The tax collector or publican was shunned and hated. At his seat in the custom house he heard the call of Jesus and the publican, the outcast, responded immediately, rose and followed Jesus. He was accepted and became one of the inner circle, one of the Twelve. Levi, also known as Matthew, was no longer alone.

— · —

The fate of the leper was tragic. He could only associate with other lepers and had to live outside of the city walls. Compelled to shout "unclean, unclean," the leper was a living parable of death and decay. With his ragged garments, his bare head, and his covered lip, he appeared like one from another world. In his desperation — or was it courage inspired by faith — one leper broke through the barriers of the law, approached the master, pleaded for compassion and did not come in vain. Jesus touched him. He broke the ceremonial law in the name of compassion. His words "I will, be clean" are authoritative and the leper is restored to the society of men. His isolation has ended. Life begins anew.

— - —

Quiet desperation had gripped the man who for thirty-eight years waited to be healed. In response to a question he said: I have no man. Seemingly no one cared. Then Jesus came, healed the invalid and slipped away. Someone had finally cared.

— - —

The wealthy tax collector suffered social ostracism. No one cared to be the guest of a man who was "a sinner." Zacchaeus had learned not to invite people. He knew better. His position as the chief tax collector made him rich and left him lonely. Jesus stopped and invited himself: I must stay at your house today. He was received joyfully. Zacchaeus was no longer alone.

— - —

To be misunderstood, to sense distrust, to be unable to communicate in depth, such was the experience of Jesus who had a profound knowledge of men, and would not trust himself to them. Betrayed by one, he was ultimately forsaken by all. Jesus understands the meaning of loneliness. The Psalmist knew that "the Lord is near to the broken-hearted, and saves the crushed in spirit." It is precisely in the moment of despair that God is near. What God said of old to Israel is still true today "I know the plans I have for you ... plans for welfare and not for evil, to give you a future and a hope." The plan is concrete, the future is positive, futility is conquered. To think that God really has a plan for my life gives it a new dimension.

The parable of the talents is a solemn warning to the average man. He who had received five talents was aware of his God-given ability and produced accordingly. But the man equipped with one talent — the vast majority of people — dug a hole in the ground and hid the master's money. Fear of failure, an exaggerated notion of his own insignificance paralyzed the one-talent man. But Jesus added that each man has at least one talent and that each one receives according to his ability. The challenge to discover and use the talent, the realization that something is expected of each and every one breaks the sense of uselessness and boredom. There is a future and a hope.

One of the great organists of Germany was more than reluctant to yield the key to his magnificent organ to anyone else on the assumption that no one could do justice to the instrument. The persistence of a young man who begged for permission to play it finally paid off. The master allowed it reluctantly. He decided to remain in the church, hiding behind a pillar to hear the young man play. Within moments the old master was entranced. Indeed, the young man played with extraordinary feeling, interpreting with great sensitivity, alternately giving expression to aspiration, jubilation, triumph and sadness. Finally the old organist exclaimed: I had no idea that my organ could yield such tones and harmony. The one who played that day was no less than Johann Sebastian Bach.

It is only when we turn the keys over to God, allowing him to unlock our potential and to use our talent that we can discover the ultimate possibilities of our own lives. There is a divine plan, a future and a hope. Amos punctured the unripe fruit of the sycamore tree when he responded to God's prophetic call and the shepherd of Tekoa became the mouthpiece of God. Gideon, the youngest of the family of a weak clan became the liberator of Israel. The gift of the lad who offered the five loaves of bread and the two fish was used mightily.

But frustration, a sense of insignificance and loneliness, does not only grip the average person. The man with multiple talents, the leader, the intellectual, no one is a stranger to loneliness. It is good to know that God cares, that Jesus called Levi, healed the invalids, and pitied the lonely widow. It is important to realize at the outset that Jesus understands and that a future and a hope are part of God's plan for every man. But the phenomenon of loneliness is so universal and powerful that a careful investigation from a Christian perspective is necessary to discover the cause and cure of loneliness.

2

THE BURDEN OF
LONELINESS

Loneliness is so widespread it almost seems to be part of the normal situation, a necessary ingredient of life. A new awareness of the insecurity of everything human has increased a sense of rootlessness and isolation. The sophisticated speak of alienation; most people are simply lonely.

The young are lonely because they are misunderstood, the old are lonely because friends pass on, the middle-aged are lonely because life seems meaningless. Man has become a problem to himself.

Communication facilities improve, but there is no dialogue. Meaningful sharing is rare. We have information without inspiration, conversation without communication, togetherness without communion. Each man remains in isolation.

We have shifted from a rural to an urban society and from metropolis to megalopolis, but compactness only results in a higher density per square mile and increased tension. Contacts remain impersonal. There is much concern for the masses, but little interest in the individual. Man is estranged from man. Loneliness is not diminished. Quiet desperation prevails.

Outer space is conquered, inner distance remains. Inner space is analyzed and in the process the person is dissected like a corpse. The volume of sound takes gigantic proportions and noise becomes a national problem, but harmony is lost and dissonance is amplified. Primitive, atonal, tuneless articulations result in cacophonia shattering the eardrums. Man remains homeless, immersed in silence. No bridge extends outward to another person. The cry for understanding only results in depression when the only answer consists of an empty reverberating echo. The feeling of alienation persists.

Perhaps the picture is overdrawn, the paradoxes too intense. The contradictions are less acute and reality not quite so bleak. Loneliness has always afflicted humanity and there is nothing new under the sun. Perhaps we are a generation of hypochondriacs, overly conscious of our problems because so much attention has been focused on psychology, sociology and all the other branches of science primarily concerned with man.

Over one hundred years ago Alexis de Tocqueville,

in his penetrating analysis of democracy made the
shrewd observation that individualism throws every
man back forever upon himself alone and threatens in
the end to confine him entirely within the solitude of
his own heart. This thought is echoed by John Cowper
Powys who wrote in 1933: "Every human being is alone
in the core of the mind. When we are born we cry; and
that cry is the cry of loneliness. Thus it is with children.
Thus it is with the growing youth. And the older we
grow the lonelier we grow."[1]

Loneliness is not a new disease. Under the title *Lonely Americans,* R. W. Brown summarized the lives of
such celebrities as Charles William Eliot (1834-1926)
president of Harvard, James McNeill Whistler (1834-
1903) whose paintings are still admired, Edward Mac-
Dowell (1861-1908) who deserves a high place among
American composers and Mary Lyon (1797-1894) who
pioneered in the field of higher education for women.[2]
They all are mentioned in the Encyclopedia Britannica,
were acclaimed and famous in their lifetime, but loneliness was their common lot. Perhaps they suffered from
the loneliness of eminence which is the price of leadership. Perhaps they were only better equipped to articu-
late their experiences, to focus more sharply on the
problem, suffering more intensely the anguish and
loneliness which is the lot of every man.

The desolate figure of captain Ahab transcends time.
He stands alone in solitary grandeur, but representative
of multitudes. Melville was a close friend of Nathaniel
Hawthorne whose central theme can almost be summed
up in one single word — solitude.

Loneliness is indeed an ancient disease. Almost two
thousand years ago the pathetic cry of a paralytic,

afflicted for thirty-eight years, expressed the feeling of multitudes when he exclaimed: I have no man. The Psalmist complained in his ancient elegy: I am like a vulture of the wilderness, like an owl of the waste places; when I awake, I am like a lonely bird on the housetop. Solomon's wisdom dictated the thought that two are better than one, but woe to him who is alone when he falls and has not another to lift him up. The king-philosopher complained about the vanity, the emptiness of everything under the sun.

But it remains true that society has seldom been gripped by such a deep sense of loneliness as in our day. Prophetically announced by musicians such as Debussy and painters such as Cezanne, interpreted by authors like Camus and Kafka, loneliness has become every man's burden. It is expressed by the artist but not limited to him.

The blues arose on popular soil. Depression, trouble, resentment or solitude is the dominant motif. The lyrics of many songs express the same mood. Eleanor Rigby is quite typical:

> Ah look at all the lonely people!
> Eleanor Rigby, picks up the rice in the church where a wedding has been, — lives in a dream.
> Waits at the window, wearing the face that she keeps in a jar by the door, who is it for?
> All the lonely people, where do they all come from? All the lonely people, where do they all belong?
> Father McKenzie, writing the words of a sermon that no one will hear, — no one comes near. Look at him working, darning his socks in the

night when there's nobody there, what does he care?

Eleanor Rigby, died in the church and was buried along with her name, — nobody came. Father McKenzie, wiping the dirt from his hands as he walks from the grave, no one was saved.

All the lonely people, where do they all come from? All the lonely people, where do they all belong?

Painters have expressed the theme of alienation and estrangement. Distortion and dislocation of human shapes are the order of the day. The clown, frequently painted, is a fit symbol of alienation. He is at the margin of society, an outcast. His actions are comical because he pretends to view reality differently, sees chairs and tables which are non-existent. The clown is absurdity expressed in painting.

As might be expected, despair, loneliness and related moods abound in contemporary authors. Thomas Wolfe endeavors to express the experience of human loneliness because "the whole conviction of my life now rests upon the belief that loneliness, far from being a rare and curious phenomenon, peculiar to myself and to a few other solitary men, is the central and inevitable fact of human existence. When we examine the moments, acts, and statements of all kinds of people — not only the grief and ecstasy of the greatest poets, but also the huge unhappiness of the average soul, as evidenced by the innumerable strident words of abuse, hatred, contempt, mistrust, and scorn that forever grate upon our ears as the manswarm passes us in the streets — we find, I think that they are all suffering from the same thing. The final cause of their complaint is loneliness."[3]

The same accent is heard in *Of Men and Mice*. Curley's wife complains: I got nobody to talk to. I got nobody to be with...I want to see somebody. Just see 'em and talk to 'em. Crooks, the Negro stable buck complains to Lennie: A guy needs somebody — to be near him...a guy goes nuts if he ain't got nobody. Don't make no difference who the guy is, long's he's with you...I tell ya a guy gets lonely an' he gets sick.

No one has handled the topic of loneliness and alienation more frequently and with greater expertise than Franz Kafka. The opening sentence of *Metamorphosis* is revealing: "As George Samsa awoke one morning from uneasy dreams he found himself transformed in his bed into a gigantic insect." In one lapidary sentence the existential situation is present. There is a sudden awareness — "one morning" — that the reality of the human condition — awaking from "uneasy dreams" — is one of profound alienation — "transformed into an insect." Few images could better express the poignant feeling of isolation and estrangement. George Samsa is alone.

The same note is heard in Camus. The opening sentence of *The Stranger* is deliberately shocking, almost brutal in its simplicity: "Mother died today. Or, maybe yesterday; I can't be sure." The hero is unrelated to anyone or anything. He is detached, alone. His life is geared to the immediate, the here and now, devoid of transcendence, devoid of significance.

Over and over again we are told that "despite all the talk that swirls around us, we are locked in a lonely prison. It is a secret and special place, a place for our own protection, yet a place of anxieties and fears, where the loneliness can be intolerable, unless we find God there."[4]

The words of Ruth Lewin in *The Shoes of the Fisherman* express the feeling of millions: "When I reached the core of myself, I knew that I should find it empty. I should not only be alone, but hollow as well, because I had built a God in my own image and then destroyed Him, and there was no one to take His place. I must live in a desert, without identity, without purpose, since even if there were a God, I could not accept Him because I had not paid for His presence."[5]

In his autobiography Bertrand Russell speaks of "that terrible loneliness in which one shivering consciousness looks over the rim of the world into the cold unfathomable lifeless abyss." Throughout his life the philosopher was aware of his own loneliness. "Underlying all occupations and pleasures I have felt since early youth the plain of solitude."

Emptiness is the chief problem. Many people do not know what is missing, they find it difficult to express what they feel. The sophisticated speak of alienation. Others simply admit to loneliness. All feel an inner void and an outer confusion and the burden of loneliness.

1. Powys, John Cowper: *A Philosophy of Solitude*, Simon and Schuster, New York, 1933, p. 37.
2. Brown, Rollo Walter: *Lonely Americans*, Coward-McCann, Inc. New York, 1929.
3. Wolfe, Thomas: *The Hills Beyond,* The Sun Dial Press, New York, 1943, p. 186.
4. Holmes, Marjorie: *I've Got To Talk To Somebody, God,* Doubleday & Co., New York, 1969, p. XVI.
5. West, Morris: *The Shoes of the Fisherman*, Dell Publishing Co., New York, 1968, p. 76.

3

THE CAUSES OF
LONELINESS

PSYCHIATRIC ANALYSIS

   As might be anticipated, many psychiatrists declare
that it all began in infancy, with the child in the crib.
The baby is quiet, "serene and satisfied despite its precarious weakness, and despite a total dependence on
others. Unaware and unappreciative of the support of
the outside world, it perceives the need for food, and it
is fed. The child need not toil or bother about living
wages — all it has to do is to whimper, or to squirm for

a moment; yet if it could think or talk it would be convinced that it is omnipotent, because it always gets what it wants when it wants it."[1]

It is at this point that the psychiatrist discovers the seed of megalomania, of infantile feelings of omnipotence. From the crib "the omnipotent baby peacefully rules the world with serene mastery. It is alone mostly, if not only, when it is asleep. During its waking hours it is always observed by mother or nurse; it is played with, amused, taken care of, attended to, talked to, cuddled and otherwise made to feel that the universe is ready to serve its pleasure."[2] Naturally the conviction grows that life is nothing else but being loved and admired and inevitably self-centeredness and self-admiration follow. In other words, megalomania produces narcissism. The word narcissism means self-centeredness and is derived from the myth of Narcissus, a handsome youth who saw his own image in a pool and fell so deeply in love with it that he was unable to love anyone else.

In an atmosphere of megalomania, under the illusion of omnipotence, any obstacle is deeply resented. If the baby's feeding schedule is not properly observed, the infant shows all the external earmarks of suffering. The discovery is quickly made that it pays to struggle, to squirm, to kick and to be angry. Food is obtained. The conquest of the world is achieved through hostility and aggression. Turned outward, such aggression appears as hatred; turned inward it appears as self-depreciation, depression and suicidal tendencies. Loneliness results from such aggressive feelings be they turned outward or inward.

The solution is hardly to starve the infant, but perhaps a disciplinary delay would be wholesome. Psychiatrists hasten to assure us that such delays would only cause anxieties, feelings of deprivation and isolation, which in turn would lay the foundation for the very evils just considered.

Other psychiatrists hold different views. They simply assume that all babies are naturally self-centered, that they live as if the whole world consisted only of things, with themselves as the unique being at the center of everything. They are only concerned with themselves and the gratification of their desires. Gradually the child becomes aware of other persons and develops powers of communication, enabling him to exchange love with his parents. But if the affection is not balanced, insufficient or too demanding, too exclusive or possessive, the child's power of communication is damaged. He will grow up in painful isolation, incapable of coming out of his shell to give friendliness or to love others, unable to accept love, full of fear, distrusting everyone and feeling alone. In this perspective, loneliness is essentially a failure of communication.

If the relation to other people engenders confidence and affords pleasure, then the child will tend to be outgoing and friendly. He will meet people readily and make friends easily. If early relationships have failed to give him a large measure of security, then his reaction to strangers will be timid, self-conscious and suspicious. The unloved child is the lonely child who too often grows into a lonely adult. Lack of approval is interpreted as rejection. Lack of acceptance leads to an experience of basic anxiety and early the child moves away from himself, since he is not good enough to be loved.

Much emphasis is placed on being socially accepted. It is a mark of prestige. Social success is so significant that at times the question "Am I successful" is equated with "Am I loved"? As Riesman expressed it in *The Lonely Crowd,* we are essentially other-directed, seeking and demanding approval. "What is common to all other-directed persons is that their contemporaries are the source of direction for the individual — either those known to him or those with whom he is indirectly acquainted, through friends and through the mass media ... While all people want and need to be liked by some of the people some of the time, it is only the modern other-directed types who make this their chief source of direction and chief area of sensitivity ... Approval itself, irrespective of content, becomes almost the only unequivocal good in this situation: one makes good when one is approved of."[3] What real or imaginary rejection means in such a situation can only be surmised, but withdrawal and loneliness would certainly be part of the ensuing result.

On the other hand, the child which is spoiled, over-loved, has similar handicaps. Accustomed to receiving the lion's share of attention and affection, he really expects too much from others. He finds it difficult to make new friends outside of his adoring home circle.

There are other viewpoints. It has been suggested that some personality types are simply predisposed toward loneliness. They suffer from a sense of inferiority, from self-preoccupation and a feeling of being unappreciated. They experience themselves as lost, orphaned, alone. It has been suggested that rugged individualism compels each man to maintain a defensive hostility to everyone else. Tournier advocates that "fear breeds loneliness and conflict; loneliness and conflict breed fear. To heal the world, we must give men an answer to fear and restore among them the sense of community."[4]

One other thought. We may be suffering from cosmic discouragement, from a conviction regarding our own insignificance in the light of the immense size of the universe. If an ancient writer saw the nations as a drop in a bucket or as dust on the scales, a modern author is conscious of the exceedingly small dimensions of the bucket and the scales. The ancient question is echoed once more: When I look at the heavens, the moon and the stars, what is man ... Lightyears, galaxies, nebulae, nuclei, quasars, stars, space ... and man seems to shrink into insignificance, gripped by cosmic despair. His fini tude has become oppressive, his limitations provoke questions, the crushing size of the universe threatens the role of man. He remains alone in a gigantic universe, isolated in space.

In *Death of a Salesman,* the key character lives in hope of obtaining the approval of his peers. He is seldom free from anxiety, fearful that approval might be withheld. To be "well-liked" was the aim of his life. Willie tried to compensate for his failures by dreams of personal popularity, the success of his sons and the approval of his company. He was unable to face failure and withdrew into fantasy and ultimate self-destruction.

At times it almost appears that the dice are loaded against humanity. Self-relatedness is necessary but unavoidably leads to loneliness. The concept of fellowship is diminished and world-relatedness impaired. Man lives in isolation. On the other hand, participation in and with persons and things can lead to a loss of in-

dividuality, a price too great to pay. Man is caught in
the dilemma — in the center of the parodox — and remains alone. He either remains locked up within himself, suffering estrangement or submerges himself into
the collective, suffering absorption.

The psychiatrist has triumphed, the analysis is complete, the dissection is finished, the postmortem concluded and, depending on the viewpoint, the victim
has collapsed, is pronounced incurable, or dead. Man
remains alone.

HISTORIC PERSPECTIVES

Some historians opt for a different thesis. They suggest that the widespread feeling of loneliness is due to
the contemporary situation, a necessary adjunct of our
historic moment. Arnold Toynbee feels that the acceleration of change in recent years is beyond the
capacity of society to accept, or the human psyche to
tolerate. We are living through a period of upheaval
when every tradition is challenged and every institution questioned. This is a traumatic experience, resulting in disorientation. Even as an individual suffers from
culture shock when moving into a new and foreign
civilization, so, it would seem, society suffers from a
massive form of culture shock due to swift transitions.
Naturally one would feel lost and lonely in such an
ambiance. Loneliness is all-pervading because it is
necessitated by the contemporary atmosphere. It can
safely be assumed that the great social shifts in recent
centuries have left a mark upon society and that the
word loneliness is imprinted in indelible ink upon
everyone. Estrangement is the word of the hour.

In the words of Paul Tournier "formerly, man was
controlled by social class: the family, the indissolubility

of the marital bonds plus the filial respect imposed by tradition, the intimacy reigning in the craftsman's shop ... and especially the community of faith and of moral, spiritual and social ideas brought about by the church — all these gave a framework to individual life."[5] Medieval man saw himself as a member of a race, a people, a party, a family or a corporation. He felt secure within a definite framework. Customs and skills were passed on from generation to generation. Gradually these concrete structures of life eroded. Family links and faith lapsed. With the Renaissance, the individual emerged. Society was atomized and everything moved toward differentiation, specialization, segregation and stratification. These are all isolating factors, not bad in themselves, but divisive without a centrifugal force strong enough to offset their potentially disruptive effect.

With Descartes' dictum: "I think therefore I am," the individual has become the ultimate reality. He sets out to prove his own existence, considers everything in terms of himself and assumes that his life is totally autonomous. At best, God is relegated to the role of prime mover, at worst to oblivion. God is dead — man is alone. As William Barrett sees it: "The central fact of modern history in the West — by which we mean the long period from the end of the Middle Ages to the present — is unquestionably the decline of religion."[6] Man has come of age. History shows that now more than ever man is irrevocably alone. At this point, historians and sociologists share the same conviction and confirm each other.

That accelerated change characterizes our era can hardly be denied. At the same time the historian may well underestimate the resilience and flexibility of man. Who can measure man's adaptability? By what standard can anyone declare what is too much or too rapid? Tillich would answer that the historical appearance of the experience of emptiness and loneliness is possible only because of their universal presence. "Estrangment is a quality of the structure of existence, but the way in which estrangement is predominantly manifest is a matter of history."[7]

It is quite true that response to change was different during the ages of faith. When a farmer's crop was destroyed by hail he suffered loss but recognized the hand of God and accepted the disaster as part of God's plan for his life. Today's farmer would only see a natural event in such a destructive hail storm, conditioned by atmospheric disturbances. He now has a scientific explanation, but lost the meaning of the event.

In the past, too, there was great suffering. Pestilence raged along with hunger and barbarian invasions inundated the land. Today the decisions of life and death appear to be in the hands of a few people who control the atom bomb or international politics. Yet in some way there is more material security in our generation through such benefits as unemployment compensation, pension plans, annuities, social security, etc. Modern insecurity may not be conditioned as much by a changing environment as a modified philosophic outlook, a different viewpoint regarding life and death. Life may be secure but meaningless, change may be relentless but progress impeded and man remains alienated because the meaning of life eludes him and a sense of disorientation prevails.

It is a striking fact that loneliness is not limited to highly industrial societies with a marked degree of change. In Africa, transitions are inevitable but slow. The African must decide between the old and the new. If the old is still dominant, the new is certainly more powerful. In *The Lonely African*, Collin M. Turnbull states the problem succinctly: "There is a void in the life of the African, a spiritual emptiness, divorced as he is from each world, standing in between, torn in both directions. To go forward is to abandon the past in which the roots of his being have their nourishment; to go backward is to cut himself off from the future, for there is no doubt about where the future lies."[8] Emptiness and loneliness are universal afflictions, be they mild or severe. Regardless of change or fixity, in spite of fluid or rigid norms, loneliness is ubiquitous, deeply experienced in every nation and across every century.

SOCIOLOGICAL CONJECTURES

The sociologist brings a different insight to the problem of loneliness. He sees man as a victim of circumstances beyond his control.

Science is the dominant factor in our day and the scientific attitude demands detachment, objectivity. Inevitably man is seen in isolation, unrelated and thereby confirmed in his loneliness. In man's confrontation with nature the key word is control, i.e., power. The relation is not one of integration but more nearly one of antagonism. Man feels no longer at home in the world. At best, the cosmos is neutral. At the worst, man is seen as the victim of a cosmic catastrophy flung into an alien universe to which he is bound by nothing. The evolutionary idea of the survival of the fittest sees everything in terms of struggle and antagonism and has destroyed the sense of oneness between man and his world. Man is a stranger in his own environment. Unavoidably the scientific attitude isolates and alienates. Science leaves intact the ultimate and decisive questions, the dramatic questions: Where does the world come from and where is it going? What is the supreme power of the cosmos and the essential meaning of life?

Science seeks definitions. Man is seen in a test tube, analyzed and defined. He is placed into categories and evaluated by comparison. He becomes a statistic and appears to be no more than an agglomeration of functions. Science has triumphed. The classification is complete. "Every identification carries with it certain labels — professor, honor student, husband, wife, president, secretary, Negro, white, doctor, teacher, Republican, Democrat, excellent, average. Through these labels and through other classifications we come to know about the person; we come to know his place in the hierarchy. In the various institutions of society — the family, the school, the church, business, industry, and government — we ask questions that will help us to label and classify — name, address, telephone number, marital status, education, and much, much more. But data that identify masses of people tell us nothing of the real person behind the data — his interests, his perceptions, his feelings, what significance various social, economic ,and psychological factors have in his everyday world; these facts tell us nothing of the real meaning of his existence."[9] The definition is precise — and we are left with the stifling impression of sadness which is produced by this functionalized world.

In spite of an apparent contradiction, there is a strange but fascinating correlation between the *optimism* of technical progress and the philosophy of *despair* which has gripped our generation. For many a philosopher absurdity is the key word which best summarizes the human condition. Sartre speaks of nausea and for him all of life tends towards gooeyness. Man is alienated, fundamentally alone and there is no exit.

Perhaps technology is the culprit. Technology is man's effort to obtain things he needs but which are not found in nature. Through technology man improves nature for the satisfaction of his necessities and desires. Man is unwilling to resign himself to the situation in which he finds himself, to submit passively to his environment. He reacts, and this reaction alters nature — be it as small a change as a stone transformed into a flintstone. This is the beginning of technology. Man builds his own environment, an artificial nature, which is interposed between man and original nature. In this sense, technology estranges man from his own environment, introducing him into a secondary environment wherein he is both at home and alienated. Nature imposes necessity on man and he responds creatively by transforming nature. This is his original calling. God said: subdue the earth ... have dominion. So man created a supernature, interposed between himself and original nature. Reaction took the place of resignation.

If nature offered man nothing but facilities for his existence the being of man would fully coincide with that of nature. Such is the case of the stone. On the other hand, if nature offered man nothing but difficulties, there would be total antagonism between man and nature and existence would be impossible. In fact, the surrounding world offers both facilities and difficulties. As a result, existence is a struggle causing tension. Technical inventions are manifestations of man's power, of his place in the world. Each step in the technological progress bears witness to man's creativity and must be recognized as good and valuable. But technical progress does not only testify to man's strength and power over nature; it not only liberates, but also mechanizes human life and gives man the image and semblance of a machine.

Dostoevski raised the question: What joy will man derive from functioning according to a timetable? How sad when man is compelled to prove to himself every minute that he is a man and not a piano key. It almost appears as if the means had crushed the ends. Sartre's story illuminates the issue: When I enter a café, the first thing I perceive are implements such as tables, seats, glasses and dishes. The end in view is the customer — or at least so it appears. In reality everything is topsy-turvey. Here for example is a door, complete with hinges, latch and lock. It is bolted and when I finally obtain a key to open it, I discover that behind the door is a wall. Finally I sit down and order a cup of coffee. "The waiter makes me repeat the order three times and repeats it himself to avoid any possibility of error. He dashes off and repeats my order to a second waiter, who notes it down in a little book and transmits it to a third waiter. Finally, a fourth waiter comes back and, putting an inkwell on my table, says 'There you are.' 'But,' I say, 'I ordered a cup of coffee.' 'That's right,' he says, as he walks off."[10] Man is crushed by the technological means which he has created. They no longer serve their proper end — man. Technology triumphs and man is forgotten, alone.

Other social scientists have highlighted different issues. Ours is a post-industrial society, an economy in which the production of material goods is being replaced by the creation and supply of services as a dominant form of economic activity. It is estimated that by 1975, seventy-five percent of the gross national product will be produced by 200 corporations. The vastness of such organizations on the one hand and the extreme specialization with the resulting division of labor on the other hand prevent single indviduals from a total over-view. This again leads to isolation and alienation.

It is suggested that adaptability and conformity are more essential ingredients than creativity and individuality. After all, it is absolutely necessary to get along with fellow workers on the job, with corporate officers, with the management and the corporation. Other people are treated as commodities, with a well-measured degree of friendliness in a purely utilitarian spirit. Relationships are superficial. Distance and indifference prevail.

Before the great industrial revolution, almost everything was on a human scale. It was easy for an apprentice to find a high degree of cohesiveness in the small family-owned enterprise. The master appeared as a benevolent father, regardless of his character. This framework has been lost. Today the individual is confronted with an anonymous, faceless, gigantic corporation.

Modern mobility may at first appear as a tremendous gain, but it may have increased loneliness. In previous eras the entire tribe moved, but the modern industrial nomad does not move within the solid structure of the clan or family. He takes the road alone or moves with his small family, following changing economic conditions or compelled by corporate decision. Permanent links, deep roots would only impede progress. Relationships are deliberately superficial. Contact would be a better word. Men touch each other like two rocks but no vital link is established, no spark ignites; dynamic relationships are absent. Ties are not intense. Associations are formal, contractual. There is an absence of trust and no sense of belonging. The modern nomad is detached, he lives in deep isolation and remains alone.

Such isolation seems contradicted by the population explosion and the rapid development of huge metropolitan areas; but the agglomeration of people has only increased the problem of loneliness. The average U.S. citizen is exposed to 650 - 1500 advertising impressions every single day. It is no mean achievement to survive this constant barrage. In order to retain a degree of sanity, it is important to screen and select. This process becomes automatic. Since advertising is concentrated in urban centers, people in the cities become more cynical, compelled as they are to protect themselves against numerous appeals. It is necessary to become blasé, to register nothing, to ignore everything, to shut off emotions. The avalanche of communication defeats its own purpose and man withdraws into anonymity and matter-of-factness.

The intellectual approach predominates, the emotional life is dwarfed. In some sense the intellect is most remote from the depth of the personality. Life becomes calculative, the world is transformed into an arithmetic problem and everything is impersonal and reserved, if not downright hostile. Indeed, in city life the struggle with nature for survival has been transformed into conflict with other human beings for economic survival. Communication abounds, but much is ignored and some is actually negative. Communication facilities are better than ever, but all too often propaganda takes the place of persuasion. Mass media are used to create a standardized mind, necessary for mass production and mass consumption. For most people life, in spite of its mobility, has become monotonous but efficient, dull but safe. Patterns are fixed, boredom prevails. Creativity is stifled and new ideas are rejected. Security is achieved but life remains hollow, empty.

In recent years, new prominence has been given to what Martin Buber called, the I-Thou relationship. According to him, all *experiences* belong to the world of I-It and all *relationships* to the world of I-Thou. In the first case, there is perception and experience, but no real connection. It is true that without *It* (experiences) man cannot live, but he who lives with *It* alone (without genuine relationships) is not a man. Self consciousness is developed through genuine interaction on a I-Thou level. In the very measure that this interaction diminishes, loss of identity increases. Utimately, failing to achieve meaningful relationships with others, one is almost deprived of part of oneself. Because so many of our relationships are purely functional, mere connections or contacts, devoid of deep involvement, we may indeed suffer an identity crisis resulting in loneliness.

Mobility, urbanization, technology, specialization, our scientific environment, each factor contributes to the problem of loneliness. Thus speaks the sociologist. Be it mass-media or megalopolis, lack of religion or of relatedness, technology or absurdity, empty communication or rapid transformation, all sociologists agree that loneliness is widespread— few agree on the actual cause. A deep sense of isolation is found among the brilliant and the ignorant, in all classes of society, regardless of creed or color. Multitudes feel estranged from the world and from other men. Homeless and alien, man remains desperately alone.

The fact that so many divergent opinions are offered by sociologists would be enough to make anyone suspicious. Their explanations are superficial, touching only external facts which, although undoubtedly contributing factors, hardly explain the deep sense of alienation and isolation of our generation. "These analyses are true as far as they go, but they are fallacious if in our period of history they derive the evil of man's predicament from the structure of industrial society. Such a derivation implies the belief that changes in the structure of our society would, as such, change man's existential predicament."[11] In these words Paul Tillich warns against a superficial diagnosis of the human condition. Ours is indeed a day of unparalleled frustration and loneliness, of solitude in mass society, of fixity in spite of mobility, of monotony in megalopolis.

As might be expected, religious leaders have added to the chorus of voices. Loneliness, so they say, is due to the loss of vertical transcendence. Man now seeks transcendence on a horizontal level, i.e., in society which then becomes a determining power in his life.

Three possible reactions can set in when the concept of transcendence is lost, when God is pronounced dead:

   1. A fatigued skepticism. A passive reaction in the face of the meaningless of life. One remains

alone, waiting for death. There is no meaning. Nihilism prevails.

2. An intense vitality, a consuming energy marks life. Feverish activity, explosive action is necessary to demonstrate every moment that one is indeed alive in spite of the death of God.

3. Autonomy or a recognition of the human predicament coupled with an effort to live heroically, without crutch, in solitude. Self-manipulation through psychological insight resulting in a measure of self-control. One accepts the situation and somehow finds inner resources.

But man "knows that dark time is flowing by him like a river. The huge, dark wall of loneliness is around him now. It encloses and presses in upon him, and he cannot escape. And the cancerous plant of memory is feeding at his entrails, recalling hundreds of forgotten faces and ten thousand vanished days, until all life seems as strange and insubstantial as a dream. Time flows by him like a river, and he waits in his little room like a creature held captive by an evil spell. And he will hear, far off, the murmurous drone of the great earth, and feel that he has been forgotten, that his powers are wasting from him while the river flows, and that all his life has come to nothing. He feels that his strength is gone, his power withered, while he sits there drugged and fettered in the prison of his loneliness."[12]

3. The Causes of Loneliness
    Psychiatric Analysis
    1. Zilboorg, Gregory: *Loneliness,* in Atlantic Monthly, January 1938.
    2. Ibid
    3. Riesman, David: *The Lonely Crowd,* Yale University Press,

New Haven, 1950, pp. 22, 23, 49.
4. Tournier, Paul: *Escape from Loneliness,* Westminster Press, Philadelphia, 1962, p. 27.
   Historical Perspectives
5. Tournier, Paul: Op. cit., p. 20.
6. Barrett, W.: *Irrational Man,* Doubleday, New York, 1962, p. 24.
7. Tillich, Paul: *Systematic Theology,* Univ. of Chicago Press, 1967, vol. II, p. 74.
8. Turnbull, Collin M.: *The Lonely African,* Simon and Schuster, New York, 1962, p. 15.
   Sociological Conjectures
9. Cf. Moustakas, Clark: *Individuality and Encounter,* Howard A. Doyle, Cambridge, Mass. 1968, pp. 6-7.
10. Sartre, Jean-Paul: *Literary and Philosophical Essays,* The Macmillan Co., New York, 1965, p. 65.
11. Tillich, Paul: Op. cit. p. 74.
12. Wolfe, Thomas: Op. cit., p. 189.

4

THE CURES OF
LONELINESS

Tips for the lonely abound. There is a never-ending stream of suggestions. If loneliness cannot be cured, it can at least be alleviated — or so it seems. Perhaps the sheer volume of suggestions could assuage the pain. It is true that most of them are hollow clichés, often unsound emotionally and economically. Not everyone can travel, sell a home, move, keep busy, get a job, volunteer, speak to new people, have a full schedule, fill and kill time and so by all means avoid the feeling of emptiness and frustration.

It is quite true that in a critical moment any action can be therapeutic, but the remedy is temporary. Changes in external surroundings are not a sufficient antidote to the feeling of loneliness. Work can fill time but not the real void. To join a club may only increase the number of unassociated persons coming together. Besides, the strength that is in a man can only be learned when he is thrown upon his resources and left alone. What a man can do in conjunction with others does not test a man. Loneliness can hardly be overcome by treating other people as a means to an end, as robots, whose only function is to help me in my own need. To multiply such *I-It* relationships will only increase the sense of isolation. The occasional contact will be helpful, but it is a palliative at best and will not solve the problem on the deepest level.

To make new friends ("if necessary, learn lines in advance") may be psychologically impossible. Perhaps withdrawal increased loneliness in the first place. The problem may in part stem from the inability to make such contacts. Perhaps initial attempts were snubbed and withdrawal resulted, dulling the senses to social response and lowering expectations. It may be true that few environments are so sterile that they do not provide some opportunity for friendship, but it may precisely be the problem of the lonely individual to meet such situations constructively.

To admonish such people to overcome handicaps is easy, the analysis may be partly correct, but this hardly solves the problem. Everything has been tried and failed. Travel and art, action and contemplation, drinks and drugs or a multitude of friends. Nothing really avails. Man lives in a thickly populated world and cannot find a single man Friday. To become a member of a club or an organization without genuine relatedness or true identity is not satisfying.

Many years ago Pascal observed: As men are not able to fight against death, misery, ignorance, they have taken it into their heads, in order to be happy, not to think of them at all. The ancient French philosopher made the bold statement that all the un-happiness of men rises from one single fact, that they cannot stay quietly in their own chamber. He adds that the real reason is found in the mortal condition of man, which is so miserable that nothing comforts him when he thinks of it closely. Hence it comes, writes Pascal, that play and the society of women, war and high posts, are so sought after. Not that there is in fact any happiness in them, but we like the chase, the thrill, we need to be diverted, entertained. This is all that men have discovered to make themselves happy. Pascal concludes that men seek rest in a struggle against difficulties and when they have conquered these, rest becomes insufferable.[1] Escapism is an ancient art. If activity can be one form of flight, alcohol and drugs are another. Of course, no one would seriously suggest that loneliness can be mitigated in this fashion. Other methods of escape are more harmless but neither do they relieve the burden of loneliness. Identification with the lives of others through the television screen or the movies is merely a flight into fantasy. Loneliness is not fully conquered.

In the desperate search for solutions, group psycho-therapy has been tried. Anything to lure man out of his isolation and withdrawal. Members of special psy-chotherapy groups select a most congenial partner of the opposite sex by looking into one another's eyes to discover the one whose gaze is the most comfortable. The tactile approach is used. Partners touch each other in an effort to establish contact. People are encouraged to give free expression to their impulses, be they hostile or friendly. All reactions are accepted without questions. In an effort to break down barriers, some groups have advocated nudity on the assumption that to disrobe physically might enable one to better disrobe emotionally. Experimental groups have met. It would seem that in some cases the cure is worse than the disease.

The psychiatrist counsels confrontation instead of flight. Maybe the psychiatrist himself can help cope with the problem. Would it not be nice if something in the past could be blamed, some hereditary or environmental factors beyond my control. Is this not another form of escapism? "When we fear life, it is easier to be persuaded that our failure to confront it stems from outside interference than it is to admit that we lack the necessary courage."[2]

Perhaps it is purely subjective, a state of mind, an attitude which can be changed? Why not look upon loneliness as a positive experience? Clark Moustakas feels that loneliness is a condition of existence which leads to deeper perception, greater awareness and sensitivity, and insights into one's own being. Accept loneliness, face it, live with it, let it be! In the same view, Rollo May writes that maturity and eventual overcoming of loneliness are possible only as one courageously accepts his aloneness to begin with.[3] It would be nice if loneliness could be defeated by affirming that it is not really a problem, but the promise of a richer life.

This is a form of self-hypnosis. Theodore Bovet tells a parable to clarify the difference between the role of the preacher who proclaims the Word of God and the task of the psycho-therapist: "The non-believing psycho-therapist is like a fireman who has located and reached the heart of the flames, but who has no water in his hose; the preacher who is remote from life is like a fireman whose hose is connected to a powerful hydrant, but who is spraying the burning house from a distance, so that the water has no effect. By contrast the good pastor brings the stream of living water right into the heart of the fire, and extinguishes it."[4]

The admonitions never cease: Change jobs, join a club, be positive, become aggressive, get married, get remarried, travel, move, have fun, never be alone, use the record player, listen to the radio, watch television, enjoy the movies, read a good book, take up a hobby, pursue cultural interests, expand your horizons, play, go to church, live a little, remember sex, start working, increase leisure, develop hobbies, renew goals, volunteer — and all of these activities may temporarily remedy the pain of loneliness but they fail to meet the problem on the deepest level and do not produce the desired lasting results.

Another solution is to renounce individuality, to submerge oneself into a relation of dependency. This is a counsel of despair, psychological suicide. As submission increases, it cannot but create hostility and rebellion, with ensuing alienation and increasing loneliness. As Bonhoeffer expressed it, for man who is in disunion with God, all things are in disunion, what is and what should be, life and law, knowledge and action, idea and reality, reason and instinct, duty and inclination, conviction and advantage, necessity and freedom, exertion and genius, universal and concrete, individual and collective. Everything is at variance, in juxtaposition, in conflict. To him for whom God is dead only absurdity and alienation remain and man finds himself alone, forlorn and lonely. His absolute autonomy has become a problem. Obviously the roots of the dilemma are far deeper than most sociologists care to admit. The cure must be more radical.

Besides, what if the very individual complaining about loneliness does not really care about anyone else? What if his loneliness is self-created, due to selfishness? Or perhaps his loneliness is merely external, temporary, caused by a sudden change in situation or environment? Perhaps it is internal, rooted deep within the person, permanent till cured by total renewal. How can one make the transition from rootlessness to an integrated personality? How is it possible to find meaning and satisfaction? How can anyone move from self-rejection to self-acceptance? There are varying degrees of loneliness, different levels. Some people seem to enjoy solitude, others remain lonely in a crowd.

The suggested cures are superficial because the diagnosis is faulty. Momentary help can be obtained, but the problem is not met at the deepest level and man remains estranged and alone.

1. Pascal, Pensées: No. 139.
2. Tournier, Paul: Op. cit., p. 60.
3. Cf. Moustakas, Clark: *Loneliness,* Prentice-Hall, Englewood Cliffs, New Jersey, 1961, p. 48.
   Rollo May: *Man's Search for Himself,* New American Library, New York, 1967, p. 174.
4. Bovet, Theodore: *That They May Have Life,* Darton, Longman & Todd Ltd., 1964.

5

LEVELS OF LONELINESS

No one is immune to loneliness. The disease is seldom fatal, but always unpleasant and sometimes almost unbearable. Loneliness has no advantages. It blights people's lives — makes them feel miserable, unhappy and unwanted. There is more than one variety and it is important to distinguish different kinds of loneliness. It can be self-inflicted or due to circumstances beyond our control. It can be unavoidable, an essential part of the human condition. Loneliness should be explored on various levels.

MAN ALONE

Loneliness is frequently self-imposed. At first this may appear contradictory since the experience of loneliness is painful, negative. Self-imposed loneliness is perhaps the most soul-searing and yet the most common. It should be easily cured since full cooperation on the part of the sufferer can be expected. But it is a feeling both acute and chronic. Perhaps a feeling of self-pity is at the root of the sense of isolation. Self-pity is not easily dislodged. When life becomes all mirrors and no window, when self-preoccupation is the overriding passion, no amount of rational argument or logic will prevail.

Loneliness is often connected with feelings of rejection. It matters little whether, in fact, the person has been repudiated. The impression prevails that something is missing, that no one really cares, that one does not belong; such a deep sense of alienation may be due to self-centeredness. Of course there may be disapprobation and exclusion. The feeling may be based on fact.

Loneliness is often associated with feelings of guilt. It is true that some people have guilt complexes and enjoy the luxury of their misery. But there is enough real guilt in every human life to justify feelings of self-alienation and self-rejection.

Anyone who assumes a leadership role will experience loneliness. The leader always moves ahead of the group. He is separated by distance, insulated in space. It is a tremendous price to pay for the privilege of leadership. The voice of the prophet is not popular. He cries in the wilderness — alone. John the Baptist was beheaded and Elijah was a solitary man when he sat under the broom tree and asked God to take his life. Socrates drinks the hemlock and dies alone. The musical genius is unappreciated and the painter starves. Such loneliness may be self-imposed, but it is exacted by the task to be accomplished. The successful leader of men faces identical problems. He is afraid to share, to betray any weakness or doubt. He too is ahead of the group, adored but isolated, followed but forlorn. The teacher, the executive, the pastor, every leader regardless of the level on which he operates tastes the painful feeling of loneliness. The innovator, the creative person, anyone who opposes the status quo, the herald of a new truth shattering old prejudices, such leading personalities will always face opposition and remain alone.

In one sense man must remain alone. He must affirm his uniqueness, not with a sense of pride and haughtiness, but as an individual, as a genuine person. This too is self-inflicted, but necessary in order to establish identity and meaning. Too many lives are empty, devoid of purpose, lived in vexation and vanity. To them all things are full of weariness and futility. The philosopher-king concluded: So I hated life, because what is done under the sun was grievous to me, for all is vanity and a striving after wind. When life is aimless, pointless, absurdity and a feeling of alienation prevail. A great effort is required to overcome nihilism, to affirm life, to discover values, to find meaning and to be a person — alone, under God.

In the central depth of our being we are alone. Loneliness is a foretaste of death. In the words of Stringfellow: "Loneliness is as intimate and as common to men as death. Loneliness is a person's specific apprehension of his own death in relation to the impending death of all men and all things. Loneliness is the experience in which a man's fear of his own personal death coincides with his fright at the death of everyone and everything else. Loneliness is not a unique nor an isolated experience; on the contrary, it is the ordinary but overwhelming anxiety that all relationships are lost. Loneliness does not deny or negate the existence of lives other than the life of the lonely one, but it so vividly anticipates the death of such other lives that they are no sustenance or comfort to the life and being of the one who suffers loneliness."[1]

MAN AND MAN

If I cannot accept myself, I cannot believe that others will accept me. Self-alienation leads to social isolation. We are unable to live harmoniously with other people because we have no inner peace.

Some distinctions have to be made. To be socially isolated may simply mean that as yet few links have been established. To be lonely is to have an unwelcome feeling of lack or loss of companionship. The former is objective, an external fact. The latter is subjective, an inner feeling. The former may be circumstantial or accidental.

Besetting feelings of loneliness are quite normal in the preesnce of tragedy, deprivation, disease and death. In a strange place, away from familiar scenes and friends one is temporarily homesick. Positive and profound relationships are necessary. When we fail to form them or lose them due to circumstances beyond our control we are lonely. But regardless of the nature of the loss "long-continued loneliness after bereavement is often the mark of inner poverty. Too many people, when thrown on their own resources, discover they haven't any."[2] They retain a sense of unconnectedness and crave relationships which they are unable to construct.

It must be pointed out that quite frequently social isolation is really the absence of desired relationships, not the lack of contacts. To be lonely in a crowd is a common experience. Often the desire to receive is not matched by the willingness to give. In this area too it is more blessed to give than to receive. Out of the dark, blind, alone, John Milton wrote *Paradise Lost*. Louis Braille lost his eyesight and created the braille alphabet. From the solitude of the prison cell John Bunyan sent forth *Pilgrim's Progress* and the apostle Paul composed some of his letters to the churches. In one of his epistles, written from a Roman dungeon Paul writes: I have learned, in whatever state I am, to be content. "Josephine Butler, full of grief after losing her only child, turned to an elderly Quaker friend. Said the friend: 'God has taken to Himself her whom thou didst love. But there are many forlorn hearts who need that mother love of thine.' He quietly suggested that she visit a home for unmarried mothers. She took the girls and their problems to her heart — and became one of the foremost women of 19th-century England."[3]

Too many people complain of loneliness, of neglect, of social alienation, but are unwilling to give of themselves. Perhaps they lack the inner resources. Life is empty when it moves on a horizontal line. It is true that almost everyone rubs shoulders with other people. There are few hermits or pillar-saints. However, interest relations must be sharply distinguished from sentiment relations. The former are determined by calculation. They are means to other ends. The latter are ends in themselves and characterized by friendship and intimacy.

Impersonal associations resemble Buber's I-It situations. Other men are seen as tools and instruments to meet my needs. Motivation is purely selfish, contacts are superficial and people are simply used to satisfy personal needs. Relief is only momentary and any minute one can relapse into depression. Moments of oblivion must be prolonged at any cost. If the crowd disperses, a new group must be found rapidly. It becomes unbearable to be alone for long, alone with thoughts of anxiety, feelings of detachment and a sense of futility. Like a drowning man clings to the rescuer, caring little about the safety of the latter, even so the lonely person hopes to survive by hanging on to others, oblivious of their needs and concerned only with himself. It would almost appear as if such people had no personal life, no inner strength. They are dependent, demand to be rescued, and use everyone they meet as the rung of a ladder to escape from the pit of despair. The social swirl becomes indispensable. Radio and television fill the few moments when aloneness is unavoidable.

Friendships originate with a different purpose and move on a different level. The motive in friendship is not personal advantage, not even the gain that friendship offers in terms of intellectual development and enrichment. What is sought in friendship is fellowship, based on an inner affinity, or a degree of like-mindedness. The mutual relationship is one of esteem and confidence, of devotion and service. Friendship will not use the other person as a means of self-gratification, as a crutch, or for egotistic purposes.

In summary, the type of connection developed with other people largely depends on what is brought to the relationship and on the purpose and expectation. Interest relationships, cold and calculated, will yield numerous superficial contacts. Friendships belong to an altogether different sphere.

Some degree of social isolation may be unavoidable. This is especially true for many older persons. A recent inquiry revealed that 46 percent of widowed people said they were very or sometimes lonely. The feeling was particularly acute among those who had recently suffered the deprivation of the company of a close relative through death, illness or migration. Drastic changes, the breaking up of old and established patterns sharply increases the feeling of isolation. Aside from bereavement, recent separation from children and grandchildren is the most important reason for loneliness. But even geographic presence may not be the solution because of the generation gap. There always has been a measurable distance between parents and children. To some extent the generation gap is not new, but a novel dimension has been added. The acceleration of change is so great that a new "generation" arises every fifteen years. Biologically speaking grandchildren may be two generations removed, but if the chronological difference is one of sixty years, the psychological gap is more likely to be four generations.

It is a religious duty for children to honor their parents, but it is essential to recall that to be loved and respected the older person must contribute something

of value to the relationship, something which is en-
joyable and gives pleasure.

All too often unfortunate personality traits are ac-
centuated with age and in this sense the loneliness of
older persons is in some measure self-inflicted. The
proximity to death is another contributing factor, since
in a deep sense loneliness is a foretaste of death.

Man is a social being. Each individual is a member
of the great organism of humanity. The Creator himself implanted the desire for society into every man's
heart. But the essential loneliness of man cannot be
cured by other men who find themselves in the same
predicament. To quote William Stringfellow once
more: "To hold that one takes one's identity from the
person of another is to equate love with possession. In
any such liaison fits of jealousy are appropriate and inevitable, for each time the other's attention or affection
is drawn to somebody else, the one whose identity is
taken from that other's life is damaged. At worst the
fiction that one's identity is to be found in another is
cannibalistic, a devouring of another; at best it is a
possessive, if romantic, manipulation by one of another
in the name of love."[4]

But even when the relation is normal, positive, it remains true that no one can by any means deliver his
own brother, for ultimately man must face death alone,
and at all times man stands alone in the presence of
God.

MAN AND GOD

We have now reached the crux of the matter. It is
impossible to analyze or conquer loneliness in its subtle
forms till we face the fact that ultimately every man is
alone. Loneliness is a seemingly inextricable human

condition. There is no exception. Even godly men have felt forsaken by God. The words on the cross, "My God, my God, why hast thou forsaken me" are fittingly called the cry of dereliction. They express abandonment, a deep sense of loneliness, supreme anxiety. Jesus was entirely alone.

It is true for each and every one that in the depth of our being remains an empty place, a vacuum, a vacant room which no one else can occupy. We may well long to usher someone in, but no one comes and nobody can. At the core of our being remains a mysterious sense of isolation which cannot be bridged. It is pointless to deny it, drown it, by din and noise, analyze or sublimate it, accept it stoically or live heroically. Loneliness persists, haunts our dreams, breaks through thick layers of self-protection, enters our consciousness even though unwanted and disturbs our life. Sooner or later the barrier is broken and questions cascade like tumultuous waves, taunting, haunting, probing, persisting: Who really knows me? Who understands? Whom do I really know, deeply, intimately, completely? Everyone remains somewhat mysterious. I cannot penetrate the hidden recesses of another. Well did Paul write that: "No one can really know what anyone else is thinking, or what he is really like, except that person himself. And no one can know God's thoughts except God's own Spirit" (I Corinthians 2:11, Living New Testament). A sense of cosmic loneliness remains. There is a yearning for sympathy which is not met, cannot be filled. Man remains alone.

Loneliness is as ancient as man and as universal as his dispersion upon the face of the earth. It is characteristic of all historic ages and we must seek an adequate cause for such a universal phenomenon. Loneliness seems to be the inevitable human condition, part of the very nature of man. The question must therefore be raised: What is man? This is the basic search, the fundamental issue.

Many conflicting statements have been made about man. Opinion has oscillated from false optimism to utter despair. Hero worship and deification has alternated with base views, looking upon man as purely animal and with contempt.

> Man is a noble animal, splendid in ashes and pompous in the grave.
>
> Sir Thomas Browne

> Half dust, half deity, alike unfit to sink or soar.
>
> Byron

> Limited in his nature,
> Infinite in his desires,
> Man is a fallen god
> Who remembers the heavens.
>
> Lamartine

> Man is a reed, but a thinking reed.
>
> Pascal

> Man is a god in ruins.
>
> Emerson

Today man is frequently seen as an aggregate of powers and forces in their interaction, a biological mechanism, the product of an evolutionary process. Poets, prophets, scientists and philosophers have all tried to answer the age-old question: What is man? Of all the answers which have been furnished, the oldest one deserves renewed consideration.

According to the Bible man was created in the image and after the likeness of God. Man is seen as the apex of creation, the crowning work of God. The enormous difference between the animal world and man is illustrated vividly by the loneliness of Adam. "It is not good that man should be alone" is one of the first things God declared about man. All the animals were brought before man, who named the cattle, the birds and the beasts of the field, "but for the man there was not found a helper fit for him." In an ideal setting, surrounded by the animal world, Adam was alone. In many other ways, the Bible stresses the unique position of man. The beasts of the earth were made "according to their kind" but man in the image of God. A simple word of God was sufficient to call the animals into being, but when man was formed God "breathed into his nostrils the breath of life; and man became a living being."

The animals are the product of God's indirect method: Let the earth bring forth living creatures.... But God formed man of the dust of the ground. The contact is direct, immediate. No wonder that no companionship can be discovered for man in the animal kingdom and that Adam only recognized Eve as bone of his bones and flesh of his flesh. Both man and animals appear on the scene almost simultaneously. A definite relationship is indicated, but the main emphasis falls on the dissimilarity. It is summed up succintly in words pregnant with meaning: man was created in the image and after the likeness of God.

Theologians have debated the meaning of these words and exhausted the options. The great Christian denominations part company at this point. Some theologians have postulated a difference between the words "image" and "likeness" as well as between the prepositions "in" and "after" as used in Genesis 1:26. In this view the image is the intellectual aspect of man and the likeness the moral aspect of man. The prepositions would stress man's inborn conformity to God ("in") and his acquired conformity ("after").

Roman Catholic theologians define the "image" as man's natural capacity for religion and all the natural gifts of man, whereas the "likeness" is defined as a supernatural gift of righteousness.* In reality such distinctions between image and likeness are highly arbitrary. An image is never original. God is the archetype, man the image ... a glorious image reflecting God to the universe. God becomes visible in man who mirrors his creator. Adam was in the very image of God, a likeness as perfect as human finitude would permit. Man was a glorious being, reflecting the God of glory. Something of this divine glory is at times still visible in man and forms perhaps the basis of the false and exaggerated optimism of man regarding himself. King David raised the question: What is man that God should be mindful of him? The royal poet himself

* The traditional Roman Catholic view regarding man is most interesting. The image is the natural endowment of man such as the spirituality of the soul (i.e. man's capacity for religion) and freedom of the will. Original righteousness was a supernatural gift of God, enabling man to maintain a balance between the lower and higher tendencies. It was the *natural* tendency of the lower appetites and passions to rebel against the higher powers of reason and conscience. This tension is called concupiscence which is not sinful in itself (it is "natural"), but only when consented to by the will. To keep concupiscence in check God added the supernatural gifts (the likeness) which produced original righteousness. Through the fall of man the supernatural gift was lost and only the natural endowment remained.

furnished an answer: "thou hast made him little less than God, and does crown him with glory and honor" (Psalms 8:5).

"Glory and honor" are attributes of royalty. Man is crowned king of creation, he is the deputy of God in the world. The Hebrew word translated glory originally speaks of weightiness, importance and hence impressiveness, prestige. The other word, honor, refers to brilliancy, majesty and beauty. Together they describe the radiance and loftiness of man.

Perhaps the ancient rabbinical legends regarding man's ancestor are an echo of the biblical presentation. According to some rabbis, Adam was placed on earth as a second angel, honorable, great and glorious. His name was derived from the initials of words designating the four corners of the world. Created immortal, endowed with superhuman wisdom, his glory eclipsed the sun. His size filled the earth and his fall brought disaster. When he turned from God his size was reduced to only a hundred yards. In essence these scattered traditions express only one single thought: Adam was a glorious being! Man was at rest. He lived in harmony with the Creator, reflecting the divine glory. He was the very image of God. There was no loneliness. Man's relationship with God was unclouded. Eve was adequate companionship. The world lay before him to be subjugated and dominated. In all his relationships man experienced no break, no discontinuity, no barrier, no estrangement, no void. Toward God, toward others, toward the world there was only positive relationship, fullness, union.

Everything changed when man turned away from God. He wanted to be more than a glorious image and

aspired to be the original. Man refused to be the
shadow of God, to exhibit and represent him. He
craved to be the model, the archetype, the fountain-
head. In his desire to rise, he fell. Dissatisfied to reflect
the divine glory, anxious to exhibit his own glory he
longed to be the substance, not the shadow. He was
not willing to rule and dominate in the name of God,
but wanted to control everything in his own name.

The desire for autarchy triumphed. A dependent
relationship with God was resented. Man fell. He
yielded to doubt when he heard the words: Did God
say? He believed the caricature of God sketched by the
devil: God does not love you and for this reason will
not allow you to eat of the tree of knowledge. God is
keeping the best for himself. Man embraced the false
promise: You will be like God! The sollicitation was
heard, the thought entertained and man moved from
contemplation to action. He turned against God. Suddenly he found himself alone in the universe, severed
from God, blaming Eve, at odds with creation. Loneliness began.

The image of God was shattered, ruined. It was not
totally destroyed. If this had been the case man would
no longer have been man, but sunk to the level of an
animal. The divine image was not eradicated. Man is
still man, but not at his best. God can no longer view
creation and pronounce it "very good". Man's relationship with God is severed and barring divine initiative man will remain alone. Man has not lost the
capacity for divine likeness, but the ability to recover
it in his own strength. His will is no longer inclined
to duty, error clouds his reason, suffering becomes a

dominant emotion. The glory is lost. God has been repudiated and man is no longer without sin.

Sin is divisive. Sin separates. Immediately it split man from God, creating a chasm between them. It also separated man from his closest companion. Without delay Adam blamed Eve who in turn accused the tempter. Man himself became a divided being. From that moment on man lived in disharmony with himself, trying to serve two masters, living in spiritial schizophrenia. Doubt replaced trust. The very word *doubt* implies *double,* two, an option, a duality. Har mony is destroyed. The center is split. Man has sinned, man is divided, man is alone, man is lonely, man is lost. The glory has been extinguished. His thought is biased, his emotion unstable, his volition weak. Man is moving away from the true center of life, he is adrift, without root and foundation. Endowed with reason to discover order and to seek truth he now lives in error. Provided with volition to carry out his duty he now exists in rebellion. Able to rejoice and furnished with emotion he is now doomed to suffer. Man moves in the wrong direction, away from God. He is lost and as the Scripture puts it, dead. Indeed, severed from the author of life man is alone, i.e. dead. Sin separates and results in death. Trust unites and produces life.

But if man is at variance with himself it is because God "has put eternity into man's mind" (Ecclesiastes 3:11). Hence dissatisfaction with the present, dreams of the past and hopes of the future. Desperate efforts are made to reconquer paradise, to produce utopia, to control the world, to achieve status, to regain glory. But death is inescapable. Man is dead. Legally he lives under divine condemnation, spiritually he is separated from God and physical death is only a matter of time.

If the glorious origin of man may explain the optimistic views man entertains regarding himself, his present condition may justify the extreme gloom of other schools of thought. Existentialism, exploring the inner moods of man, has largely drawn a negative portrait. Futility, hopelessness, anxiety have become key words. The tragic condition is stressed, but it is a tragedy without heroes or martyrs, devoid of the tragic element. The world is seen as a wasteland, man as a stranger, others as enemies and there is no exit. The death of God and the centrality of man is proclaimed but the latter is deprived of glory. Man is flung into an alien universe to which he is bound by nothing.

Oscillating between a false optimism and an equally erroneous pessimism, some have succumbed to resignation and others are spurred to rebellion. The nostalgia persists. Man seeks the weight, the glory. He would like to transcend his situation, regain the glory. This aspiration is deep-seated. Technical achievements and even space exploration cannot satisfy the deepest yearning. Cultural accomplishments cannot fill the void. Even religions fail to properly link man to the infinite.

The cult of reason in search of truth does not succeed because the thinking faculty is biased. Contradictory philosophies are the prime evidence and meager result. Emotions are unstable. Mystic experiences cannot produce lasting joy. The appeal to the will creates a system of ethics but volition is weak and the distance between the ought and the actual is frightening. Man's search persists. Unfortunately much of the search is misguided. Man misses the mark.

Interestingly enough the Hebrew word usually translated sin really means to miss the mark. The implica-
tions are far-reaching. When man sins he is really taking aim, defining a target, hoping to reach the goal.
He assumes that if he could only achieve his purpose,
happiness would result. For some it is fame or status,
for others power, or property, money or esthetic satisfaction. Man is always reaching out, moving toward a
goal which promises pleasure, peace or perfection. But
even though the goal may be reached, the anticipated
satisfaction is not achieved. Genuine peace, lasting joy,
ideal conditions remain elusive. A new target is
selected, perhaps more of the same or another category,
but the end result is the same. Those who never reach
the target may retain the illusion that if only they had
succeeded in their ambition, life would be wonderful.
Meanwhile frustration is the daily diet. Others, envied
perhaps because of their achievements, have discovered that the chase and the pursuit were more exciting
than the achievement. The goal is reached but the
promised joys remain absent and new targets are
selected. Here too, frustration takes a toll.

Man misses the mark. He is always deceived and cannot reach what he really seeks. In this sense everyone
lives in a state of delusion and deception. Sin, not as
a revolt of the will, but as an error of the intellect con-
trols his life. It is the essence of worldliness to be
attached to the external, the transient and the unreal.
The apostle John spoke of the "lust of the flesh" i.e.
pleasures affecting the senses, be they coarse or re-
fined, "the lust of the eyes" i.e. attraction to the transient, the appearance of things and "the pride of life",
i.e. the unreal evaluation of man based on wealth,

prestige and similar unsubstantial criteria. Jesus
warned against the intense preoccupation and extreme
anxiety regarding the cares of the world. There is no
fulfillment in this search, only frustration and loneliness because the goal is missed and man is self-de-
ceived. Sin has triumphed.

If man's calling and destiny is to reflect the glory of
God, then every effort of man is doomed to failure as
long as the ego stands at the center of his preoccupation. The thought of eternity fills man's heart and
nothing in the created world can fill this void. Nothing in the whole universe can appease the infinite hunger for glory in the soul of man. The God-given glory
cannot be replaced by man-made honor. In the words
of Augustine: Thou hast made us for Thyself, and
the heart never rests until it finds rest in Thee.

The words of Paul admirably summarize the situation: "all have sinned and fall short of the glory of
God" (Romans 3:23). There it is in a nutshell. At
first God, the author of our existence, the source of
happiness, was at the center of man's life. God had
communicated a ray of glory to man to shine brighter
and brighter as man matured and enjoyed fellowship
with God. Man turned away from God, became the
center, lost the glory. From here on in, something
is missing. Unfulfilled aspiration characterizes man.
Everyone falls short of the glory of God, i.e. of the
glory which originates with God. Nothing else will
satisfy. It is missing, it is sought, it cannot be attained.
We all "fall short", i.e. we are reaching out but fail to
obtain and fall behind. We are deficient, destitute of
the divine glory. We live without God's approval, without the ray of glory.

Jesus echoed the same thought when he said: "How can you believe, who receive glory from one another and do not seek the glory that comes from the only God?" (John 5:44). For those whose sole interest is human ambition, faith becomes a moral impossibility. Taking pride in external glory, they become blind to the glory that comes from the only God. The evangelist expresses the same judgment when he writes of his own generation that "they loved the praise of men more than the praise of God" (John 12:43). Actually their excessive craving for glory defeated their aim. The pursuit of praise became an obstacle to the attainment of true glory. This is truly the deceitfulness of sin, tempting, alluring, projecting vivid images, defining targets, only to obscure the truth, the ultimate reality, God himself.

The ray of divine glory can only be communicated to those who are reconciled to God, who trust him and know him through Jesus Christ.

Regardless of wealth, fame, learning, generosity, technology, achievement, position and power, the real glory is missing. Man remains alone, without God. This is the origin of loneliness on the deepest level. Ultimately the problem is metaphysical. Everything is tarnished. Man is a fugitive, a stranger, cut off from God and others, divided within himself. The words *loneliness, alone* and *one* are all interrelated in the English language and rightly so. A lonely life lacks lustre, brilliance, illumination. Life is shrouded in darkness and all the artificial illumination cannot diminish the loneliness which grips the core of our being.

Loneliness is universal because man is indissolubly

linked to God, his creator, but disregards him in his daily life. In this sense, loneliness is only an elementary expression of original sin. Sin is divisive, separates from God, cancels the divine glory in man and deceives. Substitutions are attempted but human glory can never meet man's deepest need.

It is by no means suggested that every lonely person has or can neatly analyze his feelings and reach the conclusion that something is missing, namely divine approbation. Many theories are put forward to explain the phenomenon. We have already looked at some of the suggestions made by psychiatrists and sociologists. For that matter, most lonely persons have probably not traced their loneliness to residual infantile problems, narcissism or urbanism. It is the very deceitfulness of sin to hide the basic spiritual issues involved. It is easier to blame society, parental upbringing or the selfishness of others, than to face spiritual bankruptcy.

A life lived on the horizontal plane, devoid of transcendence, concerned only with human glory remains empty, vain, lonely. But if all are in the same boat, if no one is what he ought to be, if loneliness is as universal as mankind because all have turned away from God, what is the answer? How can anyone escape? Why does loneliness affect some persons more than others? What can be done about the cure, regardless of the level at which loneliness occurs?

1. Stringfellow, William: *Loneliness, Dread and Holiness*, Christian Century, October 1962.
   Man and Man
2. Hall, Clarence W.: *How to Cope with Loneliness*, Reader's Digest, April 1956, p. 30.
3. Ibid
4. Stringfellow, Op. cit.

6

THE REMEDY

We often feel like the paralytic who, after thirty-eight years of sickness, confessed: I have no man. Surrounded by a multitude of invalids, close to one of the gates of Jerusalem through which throngs of people passed every day, the paralytic felt alone...till Jesus stopped, noticed him and spoke a healing word.

As soon as man's relationship with God was broken, man fled from the divine presence. Adam hid from God...an intolerably naive concept. Man is never really alone. He ignores God, proclaims his autonomy and sinks in despair. All this time God is there. The

ancient narrative informs us that the Lord God walked
in the garden and "called to the man." God initiated
the search and is determined not to forsake man or to
abandon him to his fate. He who inhabits eternity,
the high and lofty one, is with him who is of a con-
trite and humble spirit.

God's question, "Where are you", has reverberated
throughout history. God in search of man. The shepherd concerned for the sheep. The culmination comes
in the incarnation of God. He becomes visible in
Jesus Christ. He came to seek, to restore the broken
relationship, to communicate the divine message which
could deliver man from the burden of loneliness.

The search for human glory blinded the men of that
generation. The crucifixion was their answer to God's
manifestation of love. God is repudiated and loneliness
persists. The original position is reinforced. Man re-
jects God and remains alone.

The divine initiative of grace does not come to an
end. On condition of repentance toward God and
faith in Jesus Christ, forgiveness is offered. Man must
recognize his dependence, come to himself like the
prodigal, admit that human glory is only ersatz, a
poor substitute not meeting his need at the deepest
level. Man must come to God because God has come
to man. Forgiveness becomes the basis of a new relation,
of fellowship with God. Even as sin divides, and results in isolation and death, trust issues in union with
God generating life. The options are clear: "I have
set before you this day life and good, death and evil."

But when someone enters into a new relationship
with God through Jesus Christ, when faith and trust
predominate, the problem of loneliness is *not* auto-

matically solved. The Christian is not instantly endowed with a ray of divine glory, he is neither sinless nor innocent. He walks by faith and lives in hope. Loneliness is not completely overcome because faith is not perfect and cannot be perfect under the present circumstances. The legitimate question arises: What has been gained? To what extent is loneliness on the deepest level overcome? Does any significant change really take place? In fact, are Christians less lonely than those who seem to live without God?

When man turns to God in faith a basic change takes place. He comes under a new sovereignty and moves in a different direction. In biblical terminology the man who places his trust in Christ becomes a new creature or a new creation. This does not mean that overnight a naturally shy person becomes outgoing, a hero is transformed into a coward, or a quiet person into a flaming orator. Character does not change instantaneously. Personality traits do not vanish suddenly nor are desirable traits acquired miraculously. But the biblical word does mean that man lives under a new sovereignty and moves into a new direction. A new viewpoint predominates, a new center emerges, a new tendency appears. Christ has invaded life. God has become a reality. Some basic problems are settled. A new foundation is laid and all things are new — seen in a new light, from a different angle. The chasm is bridged, the conflict with God resolved — man is no longer alone at the deepest level. The fundamental loneliness is cured!

Paul expresses this in a few simple words: God is for us. Life is no longer lived in anxiety or isolation. Reconciliation has occurred! That God is for us becomes the basis of a new relationship, a new life. This is the triumphant conclusion of St. Paul. He describes man's alienation from God (Romans 1-3) and his reconciliation with God (Romans 4-5), and sums up the results (Romans 5-8), concluding with the rhetorical question: What then shall we say to this? He answers succinctly: God is for us. It was demonstrated at the cross and we are now assured that nothing can separate us from the love of God: death, life, things present, things to come, height, depth, nothing is able to shake the love of God manifested in Christ. God is for us!

The consciousness of God's presence — of a God who is a friend — delivers from loneliness at the deepest level. Divine approbation is enjoyed. Human glories fade and occupy no more than a legitimate and limited place. The search is ended — peace has triumphed. What Jesus said in his darkest hour becomes true for every believer: You will leave me alone; yet I am not alone, for the Father is with me. The divine promise is certain: I will not leave you desolate, bereft, alone. The practice of the presence of God becomes a matter of daily experience. The promise, I am with you always, takes on personal meaning. "I am" transcends time and "with you" transcends space. Look to Jesus Christ and be radiant.

All this does not mean that every problem is solved, but loneliness *at the deepest level* is cured. Once basic security has been achieved, once God has become the foundation of life, all else can be brought into proper perspective and balance. Of course there are disappointments; social loneliness may persist up to a point (although the fellowship of like-minded persons should make a tremendous difference); inner conflicts are not all instantly resolved. Growth is gradual but certain.

At this point it really helps to read the Scriptures, not as a mechanical device, but because the Bible fosters a sense of the presence of God. Assured that God is for us, certain declarations take on new meaning. We can now echo the words of David:

> The Lord is my shepherd,
>> I shall not want;
> he makes me lie down in green
>> pastures.
> He leads me beside still waters;
>> he restores my soul.
> He leads me in paths of righteousness
>> for his name's sake.
> Even though I walk through the
>> valley of the shadow of death,
>> I fear no evil;
> for thou art with me;
>> thy rod and thy staff,
>> they comfort me.   Psalms 23:1-4

The divine promise becomes meaningful:

> When you pass through the waters
>> I will be with you;
> and through the rivers, they shall
>> not overwhelm you;
> when you walk through fire you
>> shall not be burned
>> and the flame shall not consume you.
>>>   Isaiah 43:2

It would be pointless to multiply the quotations. Divine assurance abounds.

Prayer takes on a new dimension. It becomes genuine conversation because God is real. Fellowship with God destroys essential loneliness. Jacob was on his way to Syria. The old associations were broken up as he spent the night away from his father's house and used a stone for a pillow. Jacob dreamed that a ladder was set up on the earth and the top of it reached to heaven. The Lord stood above it. It was a remarkable emblem of the possibilities of communion between God and man. Jacob awoke, consecrated the stone he had used as a pillow and called the name of the place Bethel, i.e. the house of God. He went on his journey with renewed assurance, triumphant over the anguish of loneliness.

When a man turns to God he disavows the lie, the falsehood of human autonomy. He admits that the foundation and root of life is in God. He lives in the truth. From the Greek perspective truth is "non-concealment", it is a disclosure, a discovery. Truth is hidden but can be found through logical study and theoretical endeavor. This is the meaning of the Greek word for truth and the Greek viewpoint has dominated our culture with its scientific research, experimentation, objectivity and search for truth. The Hebrew concept is different. Here the word translated truth — of which faint echoes are heard in the English word *amen* — means that which is firm, stable, solid, permanent and therefore faithful, valid, binding. Truth is something that can be counted on because it is dependable. It is related to performance, to action. To do the truth is a typically Hebrew expression, quite foreign to Greek thought. Pilate raises the question: What is truth, searching for a system. Jesus declares: I am the truth, emphasizing a person. The Greek finds truth when he has logical proof. The Hebrew embraces truth when he finds a foundation. Rationality and dogma oppose reality and assurance. The man who comes to grips with God, humbles himself before him, trusting him, having faith in Jesus Christ — such a man lives in truth, has stability, assurance, a firm foundation. Essential loneliness is conquered, true relationships with God and man are established. God becomes the strength of life, fellowship with God a reality, and the presence of God a joyful, positive experience. In the deepest sense of the word, the Christian is no longer lonely.

7

LONELINESS OF
GODLY MEN

In *The Minister's Black Veil,* Nathaniel Hawthorne tells the extraordinary story of the Reverend Hooper, who appeared on Sunday morning wearing a veil. "Swathed about his forehead, and hanging down over his face, so low as to be shaken by his breath, Mr. Hooper had on a black veil." It was an unaccountable phenomenon which stirred the entire congregation. Only Elizabeth, engaged to the parson, finally had the courage to inquire about the mystery. The veil, so the pastor explained, was a type and a symbol of original sin and guilt. He admitted his own antipathy to the veil, which was so great that he never willingly passed before a mirror, nor stooped to drink at a still fountain. Mr. Hooper wore the veil till death, although it cast a gloom so severe that the parson was unloved and dimly feared, a man apart from men. All through life that piece of crepe had hung between him and the world: it had separated him from cheerful brotherhood and woman's love, and kept him in that saddest of all prisons, his own heart. It is true that this unusual action and ensuing gloom enabled Mr. Hooper to "sympathize with all dark affections", but at the same time the veil became a barrier, separating its bearer from all men. He admitted to Elizabeth that it was lonely and frightening to be alone behind the black veil.

Hawthorne's parable is transparent. The veil beneath which Mr. Hooper lived and died symbolized man's sinful disposition. Reconciliation with God does not automatically eliminate the problem. True, a new power invades the life of the believer. God is now at the center and man's dominating tendency gravitates toward God. Man no longer flees from God but aspires after God. The Scripture speaks of growth, development, maturity. It is precisely when God who is light, is approached that consciousness of sin increases. In the words of John, only perfect love casts out fear. In the very measure that love is not perfect, fear prevails.

Fear generates doubt and distrust. The question is raised: Is God really for me? Does he really care? In the immense extension of space does the earth really merit God's attention? Who am I among billions of people? The alternative is nihilism, nothingness. Man alone in the universe...loneliness sets in.

As long as perfect love does not prevail, as long as complete trust does not predominate, loneliness will at times assail the soul. In the final analysis loneliness is related to original sin and sin is divisive, separating man from God, from man and from himself. In spite of divine forgiveness, there will be moments of discouragement and doubt. Faith appropriates the divine promise, but only when sight replaces faith shall even the thought of loneliness be banished.

In this connection the cries and groans of godly men across the ages come as an encouragement to all who waver, fear and almost despair. Isaiah makes the blunt statement: Thou art a God who hidest thyself. The questions of the Psalmist are echoed frequently: Why dost thou hide thyself in times of trouble? Why dost thou hide thy face? If God is light he also dwells in thick, impenetrable darkness. Solomon's insight is a reminder of God's absolute transcendence and of his inscrutability. Although expressed differently, these thoughts reappear in Paul's letter to Timothy when he states that God dwells in inapproachable light. The light is blinding — darkness ensues.

Sometimes the experience of darkness and aloofness is purely subjective. The distance is created by our lack of sensitivity and fellowship with God. But there is also an aspect of God as a person and of divine activity which eludes us, goes far beyond our understanding, escapes our analysis and baffles our intellect. When God's providence appears mysterious, man may feel once again remote from God, alone, forsaken, lonely. This has been the universal experience of godly men. Such an experience is related to our finitude and therefore unavoidable. It is not easy to maintain trust when silence is the only answer, but faith can be triumphant.

There are other reasons why loneliness cannot be fully overcome. Some things should not even be attempted. Exhaustive communication is among them. It is impossible. Every idea springs from another idea and in turn gives birth to further ideas. Ideas are like rivers, ever flowing. In all communication a great deal is simply assumed and much remains unexplained because it "goes without saying". Much — perhaps the most cherished and deepest experiences — cannot be shared, is literally unspeakable. Communication is conditioned by our limitations. Communication must be true and adequate, but cannot be exhaustive. Much remains shrouded in silence. Paul speaks of the Spirit of God who intercedes for us with sighs too deep for words! We cannot express all we feel — not to God nor to men. To some extent loneliness is unavoidable due to finitude and human limitations. At the same time we do have the promise that God's Spirit, who searches the hearts of men, knows, understands and brings our inarticulate groans to God.

In some sense, each man has his own burden which he must bear alone. Some trials and troubles may be shared or removed, but some loads cannot be shaken off. "Each man will have to bear his own load" according to St. Paul. Some things we are destined to carry on our own shoulders, it is our personal burden. The Greek word used by Paul is often used to describe a man's pack. The soldier's gear is a burden and adds to the fatigue, but it is absolutely necessary for his efficiency. "We each severally have such a burden. We cannot shake it off. We cannot devolve it upon others. It was laid upon our shoulders by our commanding officer. If it is burdensome, it is necessary. Our efficiency as soldiers of Christ depends on our bearing it manfully, bearing it cheerfully. To sink under it is pusillanimous. To throw it off is rebellious... (the load) may be perhaps some physical disability... it is perhaps some defect of voice... something which prevents us from doing at all what others do, or at all events only allows us to do it with great difficulty, while they do it with ease."[1]

Such burdens may be a physical handicap or intellectual sluggishness, emotional instability or social problems. They tend to separate, to isolate, to create a sense of loneliness. The burden may be something which for some reason or other it would not be right to communicate to others, or even if communicated, they could not be of help. The isolation must be accepted but the divine presence is near. "Every man shall bear his own burden." Every man "must make up his mind to the inevitable. It is *his* burden, and *he* must bear it. It is mere waste of strength... to repine against it, to struggle under it, to try to shake it off... If he is wise, he will adjust his shoulders to the weight, and the weight to his shoulders; then he will trudge forward manfully. It will soon cease to vex and harass, if he will so treat it."[2] The load has to be carried, it is part of the equipment of Christ's soldier. But the burden is light where faith prevails.

The loneliness of godly men is exemplified by Elijah. Three times the prophet complains: I, even I only am left a prophet of the Lord. In total despair he journeys into the wilderness, sits down under a broom tree and asks that he might die. What were the reasons for his discouragement? Physical exhaustion played a role. The great crisis on Mount Carmel, his intense prayer, his lone flight and the long journey into the desert, all had contributed to Elijah's depression. Forced inactivity was another cause of dejection. In spite of strenuous efforts it seemed that the tide of Baal worship could not be stopped. Nothing more could be done since he was compelled to flee. Mental fatigue was yet another factor. The tense string needed to be relaxed. The height of rapture was equalled by the depth of depression. His sense of failure added to the burden. "I am alone" is the cry going up to heaven. All my labor is in vain. No response, no echo, no fellow, no success. Alone. The sense of loneliness is overwhelming. The desert is a fit emblem of his state of mind.

Isaiah complained that he was isolated, dwelling among an unclean nation. Jeremiah was liberated from a dungeon by an alien, an Ethiopian. When opposing popular opinion, confronting the establishment, pleading for truth and denouncing unrighteousness, loneliness will inevitably result. It is the price to be paid for leadership.

How God dealt with his despondent prophet Elijah is highly instructive. Although Elijah was hardly in the right frame of mind to relax and sleep, we read that "he lay down and slept under a broom tree." Awakened by an angelic touch, he is encouraged to eat and sleep some more. God's remedy for physical exhaustion is simple. Often discouragement could be cured in the same simple way. To the divine question

"What are you doing here Elijah?" God himself furnishes an answer. He sends the prophet on a new mission! There was work to be done in Israel and Judah and the prophetic activity had not come to an end, contrary to the morose viewpoint of Elijah. A new vision of God manifesting himself through a "still small voice" gave renewed spiritual vision and mental stimulation. Best of all, Elijah learned that his failure had not been complete. He was not alone. God was with him, spoke to him, cared for him, manifested himself. Elijah was also informed that seven thousand had never bowed before Baal. The sense of loneliness was shattered. The prophet's perspective had been too narrow, too limited. There were seven thousand times more believers than Elijah had assumed. So the prophet departed, found a disciple, cast his mantle upon him, broke the bonds of despair and triumphed over loneliness.

The words strangers and exiles graphically depict the loneliness of godly men. They speak of people who are homeless, displaced, aliens and alienated, without deep roots, wanderers, on the move. It may therefore come as a surprise and a shock that the Bible speaks of Christians in precisely those terms: strangers and exiles, aliens and pilgrims. In one sense this is to be expected. Man is estranged from God. The Christian has established a new relationship with God. If these two propositions are true, it follows inevitably that in the very measure that the gap with God is bridged, the Christian will be alienated from those who live without God. It almost seems as if man only has the choice to be alienated from God or estranged from man. Perhaps this paradox is unavoidable.

It is highly significant that Peter speaks of believers as aliens and exiles but adds the warning: Maintain good conduct among the Gentiles, so that in case they speak against you as wrongdoers, they may see your good deeds and glorify God on the day of visitation. The emphasis on good conduct is significant. Too many Christians assume that they are persecuted for righteousness' sake and have a martyr's complex, when the real cause of alienation is an impossible character. It is true that Jesus Christ was misunderstood and "as he is so are we in this world". Christian motivation may not be appreciated nor understood. Social ostracism may occasionally take place. Let the Christian be sure that such rejection is really due to that which is specifically Christian in his character and conduct. Most everyone is quick to appreciate gentleness, love, kindness, goodness, and all other Christian virtues. Still and all, relationships may be severed because of genuine Christianity. Loneliness must not inevitably result.

Peter, who stresses the fact that believers are aliens and strangers, also reminds his readers that they are chosen, called, elected. Estranged from those who oppose God, the Christian is assured of a new and permanent relationship with God. His choice and call are immutable. At the same time new social relationships are established with those who trust God. Jesus made this clear when he was informed that his mother and his brothers were outside asking for him. He replied: Who are my mother and my brothers? And looking at these around him he said: Here are my mother and brothers. Anyone who does God's will is my brother, and my sister and my mother.

The community of faith, the dynamic fellowship of the church more than makes up for the loss suffered and the social ostracism. Because the Christian has been delivered from loneliness on the deepest level, he has the strength to walk as a pilgrim, detached yet involved, alienated but elected, rejected but concerned, not of the world but in the world, serving joyfully regardless of acceptance, assured of God's love and of the fellowship of the church.

The loneliness of godly men was experienced by Job. The drama develops rapidly. Plague follows upon plague and all the waves of affliction roll over Job. He loses his possessions, his children, his health. His wife tells him to curse God. Job worships. Job's friends arrive to comfort him and share his grief. Silence prevails for seven days. Then Job cursed the day of his birth. The questions are multiplied. Why did I not die at birth, why is light given to him who is in misery? Job, in the anguish of his spirit, speaks of calamity and bitterness. He questions the righteousness of God, is anguished by the silence of God and despairs of his friends. If their silence had been helpful, their speeches were disastrous. Worthless physicians and miserable comforters, they torment Job and break him down with words, Alone, seemingly forsaken by God, misunderstood by his friends, bereft of his wealth, discouraged by his wife, Job is ultimately vindicated by God himself. The test was severe, unusual, tailored to the gigantic dimension of the man. Job did not refuse comfort but none was offered.

There are people who refuse to be comforted. It would almost seem that they enjoy their grief. Loneliness is quite normal when someone dear has died.

Job had lost his children and his grief must have been intense. The shock was even greater because death fell so suddenly. But the ancient patriarch already experienced what Paul made explicit centuries later, namely, that believers do not grieve as others do who have no hope. They sorrow, they are lonely, but never to the point of despair nor beyond measure. There is the assurance of life with God, life eternal.

It is recognized that to grieve for a lost one is largely selfish. "Refusal to be comforted is one way of keeping that person present. Loneliness becomes the last tenuous thread of our relation with that individual.... To recover from the forsakenness of loss seems disloyal —an ability to make a life without that person, despite all our vows to the contrary."[3] But when loneliness becomes a style of life it is no longer a fitting tribute to the memory of the departed, but the assumption of a dramatic role which seems to add an interesting dimension to the monotony of daily life. The unreality and selfishness of such an attitude is self-evident. The Christian perspective both of this life and the life to come should shield the believer from such role-playing and delusion. Job is dramatic, but the denouement soon comes. He sought for comfort and found none till he had a renewed vision of God.

Deprivation can produce a momentary but deeply felt sense of loss and loneliness. Perhaps someone we have known has died, a friend, relative, child, husband or wife; perhaps a position has been lost, a career come to a sudden end; perhaps a goal has been denied, an aspiration crushed, a dream shattered. The upheaval is sudden, brutal, final. Loneliness is unavoidable but not permanent, not without remedy nor without hope.

The foundation remains firm. God is still sovereign, still to be trusted, even "though I walk through the valley of the shadow of death." This was the experience of Job, it is the normal reaction of believers in the face of extreme emotional stress.

There are other reasons for the loneliness of godly men. There is the apartness of leadership. "If the leader is defined as walking ahead of the group, he is necessarily separated from the group, alone, isolated ... unoriginal followers can hardly appreciate original leadership ... every act of courage and every creative initiative tends to isolate the leader."[4] Whoever "goes first" goes, by definition, alone. This was the experience of Jesus, the leader *par excellence*.

The apostle Paul carried the same burden. Toward the end of his life, in prison once again, he writes his last letter to his disciple Timothy. The pathos of his words is unmistakable: "The first time I was brought before the judge no one was here to help me ... Erastus stayed at Corinth, and I left Trophimus sick at Miletus. Do try to be here before winter ... Please come as soon as you can. Demas ... has deserted me ... Titus has gone to Dalmatia. Luke alone is with me!" Paul asks for a coat, the books and the parchments. He longs for something to read, to study, to occupy his mind, but most of all for friendship, fellowship, for Timothy and Mark, for old acquaintances and for someone aside from Luke, to stand with him in his defense. Paul, the aged, as he calls himself, had experienced the loneliness of leadership all his life. In the closing days of his pilgrimage he longs for deep understanding, for a shrinking of the distance between the leader and

the group, for intimacy and moral support. Even books
would be helpful to shorten the passage of time.

One is involuntarily reminded of a letter written in
1535 by Tyndale, imprisoned in Vilvorde, and ad-
dressed to the Marquis of Bergen: I entreat your lord-
ship, by the Lord Jesus, that if I must remain here for
the winter you would beg the Commissary to be so
kind as to send me, from the things of mine which he
has, a warmer cap; I feel the cold painfully in my
head. Also a warmer cloak, for the cloak I have is very
thin. He has a woolen shirt of mine, if he will send
it. But most of all my Hebrew Bible, grammar and
vocabulary, that I may spend my time in that pursuit.

Leadership automatically entails a certain degree
of loneliness, but forced inactivity could aggravate the
problem immensely and produce an awareness of loneliness far beyond the normal experience. Tyndale was
burned at the stake and died triumphantly. Paul, in
the same context wherein he mentions his need for
companionship, also expresses his conviction that God
is a righteous judge and that a crown of righteousness
awaits him. He added: "The Lord stood by me and
gave me strength to proclaim the word fully." Deserted
by all, imprisoned and forcibly inactive, Paul was still
assured of God's favor and lived triumphantly. Loneliness had not become an intolerable burden. Essential
loneliness was overcome; social loneliness remained a
real factor but the foundation could not be shaken regardless of the isolation, incarceration or desertion.
The triumph of faith had sustained the leader throughout life and even in the darkest days. Shortly before
the lonely hour of death, the same faith linked Paul

to the eternal God and gave him strength to face his situation.

The loneliness of godly men is real. Sin isolates from God and creates a sense of loneliness. As long as sinless perfection has not been attained, the possibility of loneliness remains. Our human limitations do not permit exhaustive communication. Some things cannot be shared. Some burdens must be borne alone, in silence. A godly life may also be an isolating factor and we are reminded that Christians are aliens and strangers in the world. Sudden calamity does not spare the believer and the loneliness caused by death cannot be escaped. Some must pay the cost of leadership.

All this is true. These situations are unavoidable... and so is loneliness. But for the believer loneliness on the deepest level is healed. Forgiven, reconciled, accepted, God has become the foundation of life and the ray of divine glory illuminates all of existence. Faith may suffer an eclipse, but the ultimate triumph is certain. Desertion and death, ostracism and snobism, sin and suffering, burdens and bereavement, these factors are real and must be faced courageously, but they cannot separate from the love of God nor destroy the fellowship of the church. The conquest of loneliness is made easier by two additional considerations.

We are never alone. Elijah was not alone — there were seven thousand. Job was not alone — there always is "a cloud of witnesses." These graphic words were penned to remind Jewish converts that they were not alone. "Since we are surrounded by so great a cloud of witnesses, let us also lay aside every weight, and sin which clings so closely, and let us run with perseverance the race that is set before us, looking to Jesus the pioneer and perfector of our faith...." (Hebrews 12:1, 2). A dual concept is introduced here. The heroes of faith of days gone by, who are mentioned in Hebrews 11, have testified to the good results of faith. Their lives witnessed to the triumph of faith. This is the sense given by the New English Bible: With all these *witnesses to faith* around us like a cloud.... But more is involved. We are *surrounded* by the witnesses. They are spectators! The Living New Testament focuses on that aspect of the truth, "Since we have such a huge crowd of men of faith watching us from the grand-stands,...."

There is a huge crowd, a vast throng who are both witnesses to faith and spectators of our faith. There is a link between the church triumphant and militant, the church above and below. We are never alone. There is always a cloud of spectators. The stimulus of example and presence is an encouragement to run the race, to fight the battle, the eyes fixed on Jesus Christ in whose steps we walk and who never leaves us nor forsakes us. But even the cloud of witnesses fades into the background in the presence of God. The last days of Jesus illustrate his concern for the lonely and for-lorn.

A few days before the Passover feast when the tem-ple was crowded with worshippers, Jesus stood in the temple precincts. In the court of the women he noticed a widow. If the position of a woman in the Orient was precarious, the fate of a widow was desperate. And this widow was poor. She approached one of the thirteen chests and deposited her two copper coins. The lepta was the smallest coin in circulation. Out of her poverty she gave everything she had, her whole living. The

rich gave much, she gave all. But she was not unob-
served. Jesus saw the lonely poor widow and called his
disciples to him. They too were in the temple area.
Their visits were infrequent and they took advantage
of it to admire the building. Jesus calls them to focus
their attention on the widow.

The apostles exclaim: Master, look at the beautiful
stonework and the wonderful buildings! From a distance the temple appeared like a mountain covered
with snow, glistening in the sunlight, for all was over-
laid with gold. Herod had embellished the temple
with stones, some of which were twenty-five cubits
long, eight high and twelve wide. The halls, the
colonnades, the enclosures, all the buildings fascinated
the disciples. They ignored the widow. At best their
attention might have been aroused by some dignitary,
a member of the Jewish council or a distinguishd foreign visitor. Responding to their admiration of the
magnificent stones, Jesus announces the destruction
of the temple. "As for these things which you see...
there shall not be left here one stone upon another."
The temple with all its pomp and glory will be destroyed; the soul of the widow lives on forever. The
things which *you see*...you fail to see the widow,
humble, poor, alone. She was remarkable and should
have been noticed. Jesus saw her.

Perhaps an overwhelming feeling of loneliness had
gripped her in the midst of the crowd, perhaps the
heroic act of faith was her response to the trials of life.
But if she assumed that no one cared, no one observed,
no one sympathized, she was mistaken. Jesus saw the
widow...even as he saw Zacchaeus the tax collector,
the woman of ill-repute in Simon's house, Peter's

The Meaning of Loneliness

mother-in-law, the paralytic, the outcast, the lonely, the lost. The loneliness of godly men and women can never be overwhelming, nor absolute. Regardless of our situation — regardless of doubt which might temporarily eclipse God, or holiness which might alienate from some men, in spite of the presence of death and the tests of life, we are surrounded by a cloud of witnesses and live in the presence of God. Let us run the race, looking unto Jesus, because he sees us. Nothing can separate from his care and concern, no one is lost in a crowd or insulated in space. Jesus saw the widow — he sees you.

1. Lightfoot, J. B.: *Ordination Addresses and Counsels to Clergy,* Macmillan & Co., London, 1890, p. 136 ff.
2. Ibid
3. Drury, Michael: *When You Face Loneliness,* Woman's Day, April 1969.
4. Wolff, Richard: *Man At the Top,* Tyndale House Publishers, Wheaton, Illinois, 1969 pp. 71-72.

8

SOLITUDE

"I have never felt lonesome, or in the least oppressed by a sense of solitude, but once ... for an hour, I doubted if the near neighborhood of man was not essential to a serene and healthy life ... I find it wholesome to be alone the greater part of time. To be in company, even with the best, is soon wearisome and dissipating. I love to be alone. I never found the companion that was as companiable as solitude ... A man thinking or working is always alone, let him be where he will." Very few people in our day would agree with the feelings of Thoreau. As a matter of fact, Thoreau only stayed about two years at his famous residence in Walden Pond and even there he was not always alone.

Writing from a totally different perspective Martin Luther in his *Table Talks* expressed the view that "more and greater sins are committed when people are alone than when they are in society. When Eve, in paradise, walked by herself, the devil deceived her. In solitary places are committed murders, robberies, adulteries, etc.; for in solitude the devil has place and occasion to mislead people. But whosoever is in honest company is ashamed to sin, or at least has no opportunity for it; and, moreover, our Savior Christ promised: 'Where two or three are gathered together in my name, there will I be in the midst of them.'

"When king David was idle and alone, and went not out to the wars, then he fell into adultery and murder. I myself have found that I never fell into more sin than when I was alone. God has created mankind for fellowship, and not for solitariness, which is clearly proved by this strong argument: God, in the creation of the world, created man and woman, to the end that the man in the woman should have a fellow." (Paragraph 659.)

Is solitude a blessing or a curse? Should it be cultivated or avoided? Is there a via media or are we facing another paradox? There are times when we all feel like the psalmist:

My heart is in anguish within me,
the terrors of death have fallen upon me.
Fear and trembling come upon me,
and horror overwhelms me.
And I say, "O that I had wings like a dove!

I would fly away and be at rest;
yea, I would wander afar,
I would lodge in the wilderness,
I would haste to find me a shelter
from the raging wind and tempest. Psalms 55:4-8.

It may be necessary to distinguish various types of solitude. Motivation varies. There are those who voluntarily and deliberately shun togetherness. They seek solitude to follow out their own desire and enjoy the thought of ignoring mankind. The misanthrope cultivates his solitude with care and despises mankind. For others, solitude is a necessity dictated by special circumstances. "The scientist withdraws into his retreat because he, too, temporarily loses his interest in the outside world; but this is a self-imposed withdrawal, not a true loss of interest. Moreover, while he withdraws from the world, he does so because he is intensely interested in a certain piece of work — in something which is not his own little self; also, as soon as his work is done, he comes back willingly and cheerfully to the outside world. Another point to note: the solitude he seeks is not to him something unpleasant imposed on him by circumstances, — that is, the outside, — not something discouraging, impoverishing his personality and belittling his self-respect, but something welcome, comfortable, something that has in its store the enriching experience of creative work."[1] In the same vein the student, the creative person, the teacher, the preacher and many others find the solitude of the study or laboratory the necessary condition which enables them to carry out their work successfully.

Solitude has advantages. Loneliness has none. There are even pleasures in solitude. No effort has to be made to accommodate other people. Such pleasures are dangerous.

The solitary world becomes narrow, selfish and possibly a breeding ground for loneliness. This may be due to the fact that when we are alone our identity tends to lose its dimensions and to become vague in its boundaries. Only a strong sense of the presence of God can counteract this tendency.

Loneliness is negative; solitude can be positive. Loneliness has been defined as the acute, chronic, non-directed sense of aloneness that breaks down man's integration! As Tillich put it much more simply: Two words express man's aloneness. Loneliness speaks of the pain of being alone; solitude expresses the glory of being alone.

Loneliness exists when you are compelled to be alone; solitude comes into play when you choose to be alone. Solitude may reveal and increase loneliness, but this is not a necessary consequence. Solitude can indeed be a glorious experience. It was for Jesus Christ, who frequently withdrew from the crowd and went into the hills to pray.

Self-imposed solitude is so far removed from the concepts which dominate our society that anyone who spends much time alone is considered a failure. It is inconceivable to most people that anyone would actually choose to be alone. Yet, in the words of Tournier, "it may well be that the deeper experience of fellowship has as one of its necessary conditions that we first achieve a creative solitude."[2]

The Bible, as usual, presents a balanced view. The wisdom literature warns: The separatist seeketh after his own pleasure; against all that is beneficial he showeth his teeth (Delitzsch on Proverbs 18:1). The man who obstinately withdraws himself is condemned. He ignores the community, and only cherishes and pursues his own plan and pleasure. His fanatical opposition is directed against all that is useful and profitable in the aims and principles of the community. His angry snarl is well depicted in one of Shakespeare's characters who confesses:

> The midwife wonder'd, and the women cried
> 'O! Jesus bless us, he is born with teeth.'
> And so I was; which plainly signified
> That I should snarl and bite and play the dog.

The additional comment is significant:
> I have no brother, I am like no brother;
> And this word 'love,' which greybeards call divine,
> Be resident in men like one another
> And not in me: I am myself alone.*

The man who "is born with teeth" or snarls and bites will end up loveless and alone, with only limited relationships to other men. One is involuntarily reminded of Mr. Haller, the hero of *Steppenwolf,* by Herman Hesse. Mr. Haller was unsociable to a degree never before experienced in anyone else. On account of his disposition his life had drifted into loneliness which he had accepted as his destiny. He gave the impression of having come out of an alien world, from another continent. He seemed to be on the outside of everything and his life was marked by pessimism and despair. Although the author feels that in spite of this attitude the Steppenwolf was a real Christian, such be-

* The Third Part of King Henry VI, Act. 5, Sc. 6.

havior is incompatible with true Christianity. Haller
was filled with rage against this toneless, flat, normal
and sterile life. He had a mad impulse to smash something, to commit outrages, to spark rebellion. This
Kafkaesque character has been popularized by contemporary existential writers.

The Stranger by Camus is the portrait of an alienated
man who could echo the word of Shakespeare: I am myself alone. In periods of disintegration and eras of
great upheaval it is a temptation to withdraw from
society and to cultivate the "self." But man is not only
a "self," he is a complex being with relationships to
God and man. He is a son, a brother, a father, a friend,
a citizen. Stripped of all these relationships, he is no
longer man in the truest sense of the word but a mere
"self" — a hungry, hollow, shrivelled self.

St. Anthony (A.D. 250-350) was the first Christian
monk. First he withdrew to a mountain by the Nile and
later to the mountains by the Red Sea. But evil spirits
followed the anchorite into the desert, and his tempta-
tions were not diminished by his withdrawal. It remains true that it is not good for man to be alone, although it might even be worse never to be alone.

The danger of being secularized by constant involvement in social life is also real. Many are absorbed in
externals and worldliness. Their constant exposure to
society leads to a loss of individuality. This was well
expressed by Dag Hammerskjöld in Markings: "A
blown egg floats well, and sails well on every puff of
wind — light enough for such performances, since it
has become nothing but shell, with neither embryo nor
nourishment for its growth. 'A good mixer.' Without
reserve or respect for privacy, anxious to please — speech

without form, words without weight. Mere shells."[3]
The character of the mass is unconsciously adopted.
Persons and things constantly sollicit attention and the
individual is distracted. So many impressions press upon
the soul that concentration becomes impossible. Yet a
goal cannot be reached without intentness. These
pressures result in a society adrift, aimless and shiftless,
at the mercy of mass influences. The necessity therefore
arises to be alone, to shut the door and to pray.

Christians are challenged to become imitators of
Jesus Christ. His life was marked by times of withdrawal for meditation and prayer. At times he even left
the crowd and moved into isolation. Much of his time
was spent with the disciples in the midst of crowds.
But even when surrounded by multitudes, Jesus was
conscious of the one person really touching him. The
incident is well known. When a crowd thronged about
Jesus a woman came up from behind and touched the
fringe of his garment. Jesus raised the question; Who
touched me? He was in the crowd, but not of the
crowd, not submerged nor shaped by it. In the truest
sense of the word, Jesus remained himself alone.

To a large extent the inner life of our Lord remains
a mystery to us, even as the inner life of the Christian
remains a mystery to the outsider. This is precisely
what Paul meant when he wrote that our life is hidden
with God in Christ. The roots of the new life, the
foundation of the Christian, his motivation, his
strength, his action, all this remains invisible to the
outsider and puzzles him.

The process of learning has been defined as one of
contact and withdrawal. These two words adequately
describe the relationship of the Christian. He hears

both the words "Come unto Me" and "Go into all the world." At times he moves in the crowd, at others he enjoys solitude in the presence of God. It was in solitude that God spoke to Moses, to Elijah and to John the Baptist. But even when they were surrounded by throngs of people, their fellowship with God was undisturbed and uninterrupted. This was the secret of their strength. The Christian is always aware of the presence of God. Surrounded by the deafening noise of society the Christian, regardless of his activity and response, is at the same time open to God, listening and receptive.

Life in following Christ is at the same time lived for the perfecting of the community to which we belong and for our personal perfection. It is therefore necessary that an alternation take place between social life and solitude. Social life invariably leads to solitude, for how can we carry out God's will in the community if we do not in solitude unite our will with God's in prayer and contemplation. Conversely, solitude leads back to the community, for everything that is strengthened and renewed during times of solitude — love to God and man — must issue in obedience and a practical ministry to people.

In our day the admonition of Christ to "go into your room and shut the door and pray" may need the greater emphasis. Meditation is a lost art. Too many are loosing themselves in an endless round of activities, especially christian activities, and their hidden life is impoverished.

Much is a matter of temperament. Some would yield to a propensity to glorious solitude, others cherish the joys of society. A healthy balance is needed. Much depends on the special calling of God and the sphere wherein he has placed us. At all times the inner man must be cultivated in fellowship with God. The cares of the world should never be allowed to kill receptivity to the word of God. Contemplation and activity are not mutually exclusive. Paul was lifted in the third heaven and heard unutterable things; he speaks of the depth of God and glances into the mystery of God's sovereign purposes in time and eternity. Yet at the same time he undertook distant journeys by land and sea, preached, wrote, organized, collected and planted churches across the Roman Empire. Luther and Wesley showed similar characteristics. Because of the intense social pressures of our day special strength is required to be the kind of person God expects us to be, in the world but not of the world. Glorious solitude, a deep sense of the presence of God, is not only an antidote to loneliness but the foundation of strength and peace in our troubled days.

1. Zilboorg, Gregory: *Loneliness*, Atlantic Monthly, January 1938.
2. Tournier, Paul: Op. cit., p. 10.
3. Hammerskjöld, Dag: *Markings*, Alfred A. Knopf, New York, 1968, p. 39.

9

FRIENDSHIP

One of the most striking contrasts between the ancient and the modern world is the place given to friendship by moralists and religious teachers. In Aristotle's treatise on Ethics two books out of nine are devoted to the topic of friendship. These chapters form the climax of the work. Socrates and Alcibiades, Achilles and Patroclus were some of the celebrated friendships of antiquity.

Aristotle points out that friendship "is one of the things which life can least afford to be without." He adds that friendship is a necessity of human nature, but only perfect between those who are good. Utilitarian "friendships" are neither deep nor lasting. If only mutual advantage is pursued, so-called friends part as soon as the relationship is no longer profitable. True friendship has a different basis. The good man, writes Aristotle, feels toward his friend as he feels towards himself — for a friend is a second self, an alter ego. A true friend would therefore wish to share that "which forms for him the essence and aim of his existence." Aristotle's views have certain limitations, It seems that friendship is necessarily selfish, springing from a wish to realize oneself in the life of another, fed by the benefit and pleasure derived from such a relationship. Finally, friendship can only exist between equals, *"good men" on the same level of virtue.* By contrast, Christ was a friend of "sinners." Christian love seeks nothing but gives all.

The friendship of David and Jonathan is the classic example of the scriptures. The friends of Job are also famous, although they failed to comfort him. Their attitude deeply wounded Job who exclaimed: My friends scorn me ... my close friends have failed me. He pleaded with them: Have pity on me, O you my friends, for the hand of God has touched me. The high premium placed on friendship is revealed by the simple words describing Abraham's relationship with God: Abraham was called the friend of God. The words of Jesus shed a brilliant light on the topic of friendship:

> I demand that you love each other as much
> as I love you.
> And here is how to measure it — the greatest

love is shown when a person lays down his life
for his friends;
And you are My friends if you obey Me.
I no longer call you slaves, for a master doesn't
confide in his slaves; now you are My friends,
proved by the fact that I have told you everything the Father told me.　　　John 15:12-15
　　　　　　　　　　　　　Living New Testament

In various degrees the apostles were friends of Jesus.
John was especially favored. Friendships were also
formed outside the apostolic circle. Lazarus was among
them. Unfortunately even some of Jesus' friends failed
to understand him and at one point feared that he was
beside himself. The friendships of Jesus knew no social
barriers.

Man is a social being. Friendships naturally flow
from the deep-rooted desire for companionship. The
ancient words: "It is not good that man should be
alone" find an application here too. Friends, according
to the original sense of the Hebrew word, are those
who delight in one another's companionship. They
are useful to one another because each possesses gifts
which the other has not and they are agreeable to one
another because they have much in common. The
Grecian sage said: Show me your friends and I will tell
you who you are. It is true that birds of a feather flock
together. Bonds of friendship may link criminals and
conspirators but the companion of fools will suffer
harm. For this reason Solomon advised: "Make no
friendship with a man given to anger, nor go with a
wrathful man."

True friendship can only exist on the basis of religious harmony. Two cannot walk together unless

they are agreed, and this mutual consent must embrace the deepest convictions, those of the spiritual life. The maxim: "Bad company ruins good morals" remains true. Genuine friendship is only possible with like-minded persons. Only with them is a relation of esteem and love possible. The moral element is never absent.

Friendship is not a means to gain personal ends or advantages, not even in terms of intellectual development, nor as a cure for loneliness. It is true, of course, that friendship will alleviate loneliness, but this by-product should never become the underlying motive. A friend loves at all times. He is always loyal, seeks the welfare of the other person and will, therefore, if necessary, rebuke him for his faults. This is an additional reason why a basic incompatibility, especially in the area of religion, will become an insuperable obstacle to friendship.

"As in water face answereth to face, so the heart of man to man." As in a water-mirror each one beholds his own face, so out of the heart of another each one sees his own heart, i.e., he finds in the other person, the dispositions and feelings of his own heart. Even as the face is reflected in the water, so the heart of man is echoed in another.[1] In the heart of a friend we see our own character reflected, just as gazing into a still pool we see the reflection of our own face. We come to know ourselves through the sympathetic relationship of friendship. This is preeminently true in our relationship with God, but in a lesser degree of every genuine friendship. We unfold to one another, we discover our similarities and mark our differences. Because all men are of like nature and capable of the same emotions, one can pour into the heart of another that which fills and moves our own hearts and find agreement, understanding and a sympathetic echo. Certain aspects of our character which remain obscure to ourself are gradually detected when we see them in our friends. Unused faculties are brought into play.

The intellectual value of friendship is brought out in the happy saying: Iron sharpens iron, and one man sharpens another. A friendless person has a lackluster face, his talk has a dull edge and his emotions a feeble flow. But the proverb intends yet more. Friendship must operate in such a way as to sharpen the character of the other person, polish his manner, refine his culture, round off his corners. The friction may occasionally be distressing, but "faithful are the wounds of a friend." His frankness may be uttered at great personal cost, for our good rather than his.

The decisive test of real friendship comes in the day of adversity. A friend is never known till needed. In the days of calamity, in hours of loneliness, when it seems that our world falls apart, in the moment of desperate need, the real friend sticks closer than a brother. As Solomon expressed it, "The sweet exhortation of a friend from a soul capable of rendering counsel is like ointment and perfume, rejoicing the heart." When a friend is near at hand in the moment of need, he is of more service than our own brother. This was the thought of the royal philosopher when he wrote:

> Your friend, and your father's
> friend, do not forsake;
> and do not go to your brother's
> house in the day of your calamity.
>
> Proverbs 27:10

Lonely people frequently complain about their isolation and lack of friends. They long for friends but seemingly fail to discover them. Friendships are not altogether spontaneous. They must be cultivated. Friendship is of delicate growth and even when it has become robust can easily be blighted. Sometimes the results of years can be lost in a few days.

In the charming book *The Little Prince,* Antoine de Saint Exupéry describes the encounter between the little prince and a fox. The prince invites the fox to play with him, but the fox refuses because he is not tamed. Three times the little prince raises the question: "What does that mean — 'tame'?" Finally the fox answers: It is an act too often neglected. It means to establish ties. The fox further explains:

> "To me, you are still nothing more than a little boy who is just like a hundred thousand other little boys. And I have no need for you. And you, on your part, have no need of me. To you, I am nothing more than a fox like a hundred thousand other foxes. But if you tame me, then we shall need each other. To me, you will be unique in all the world. To you, I shall be unique in all the world...if you tame me it will be as if the sun came to shine on my life."

At first the little prince refused to tame the fox, feeling that he would not have enough time because he had friends to discover and a great many things to understand. The rejoinder of the fox is beautiful in its simplicity: "One only understands the things that one tames.... Men have no more time to understand anything. They buy things all ready made at the shops. But there is no shop anywhere where one can buy friendship."

Patience is needed to tame the fox and all the little prince can do at first is to sit a little closer each day to his new-found friend. When the little prince moves on and says goodbye to the fox, the latter utters a final word of wisdom: You become responsible, forever, for what you have tamed.

Friendships must be cultivated, gradually and deliberately. This demands a certain effort, a genuine concern for the other person and a willingness to shoulder responsibility. Too many people who complain about the lack of friends take no initiative to develop such a valuable relationship. Often they are too self-centered to "tame" another person, to bestow affection or to assume the responsibility.

In the era of communication the possibilities of friendship are vastly multiplied. A friend who lives twenty-five miles away can be much closer than an acquaintance close by. Distance has been conquered. The car has created a mobile society. To keep in touch by telephone is more than an empty slogan when applied to friendship. How extraordinary that genuine friendships can be maintained regardless of geographic distance because of modern inventions. An effort is required, initiative is needed, mutual acceptance and common ground are necessary prerequisites, but the intense enjoyment of Christian friendship can hardly be exaggerated. If essential loneliness is overcome when man is reconciled to God, carefully cultivated friendship triumphs over loneliness on the horizontal plane. The enthusiastic words of Emerson "A friend may well be reckoned the masterpiece of nature" are only an echo of the meditations of Sirach who declared that a faithful friend is the medicine of life.

1. Cf. F. Delitzsch's Commentary in loco and the Expositor's Bible on Proverbs Chapter 17.

10
THE SINGLE LIFE

In a recent TIME essay entitled *The Pleasures &
Pain of the Single Life,* the conclusion is reached that
"the greatest pressure on the singles is the classic one
—loneliness." On a pragmatic basis loneliness is de-
scribed as "coming back to an apartment where the
breakfast dishes are still unwashed, the morning paper
exactly where it was dropped, where nothing has
moved." The conclusion of the essay reflects the popular view that "a single girl is like a single letter in the
alphabet, waiting to mean something to someone." It
illustrates the prevailing idea that celibacy is a minor

disaster. Whenever a single person is introduced to a group, someone instinctively becomes a matchmaker. Apparently all happiness resides in marriage and life is empty without connubial bliss. But nowhere does the Bible explicitly state that the sole destiny of women is in marriage and motherhood.

There are millions of single adults, often considered the loneliest of the lonely crowd. Aside from those who have never married there are many young widows, widowers and divorced persons. The churches are flooded with single adults and relatively little is done to be of help to them. Many want to be married and should therefore be married. What better place to find a suitable mate than in the church? The organization of special young adult groups is certainly justified and whatever else can be done to make it possible for single Christian men and women to meet should be initiated.

At the same time it must be pointed out that the emphasis on marriage is exaggerated. The single person can find fullfilment. Many are single by choice. The church should react vigorously against the stigma attached to celibacy. In the early church, the situation was the reverse and celibacy was highly esteemed. The protestant reaction has moved the pendulum too far in the other direction. Some of the specific scripture references must be considered.

The words of Jesus are normative: "There are eunuchs who have been so from birth, and there are eunuchs who have been made eunuchs by men, and there are eunuchs who have made themselves eunuchs for the sake of the kingdom of heaven. He who is able to receive this, let him receive it" (Matthew 19:12).

Marriage had just been discussed. Jesus now focuses attention on the single state. He distinguishes three situations: 1) Those born with a defect. The problem is congenital. Merit or guilt is not involved. By extension one might include all those who have no tendency toward marriage, be it through natural incapacity or inaptitude. 2) A group of persons deprived artificially, emasculated and thereby prevented from marrying. By extension one might include all who through one form or other of pressure and compulsion are not free to engage in marriage. Misfortune and/or guilt are involved. 3) A voluntary abstinence from marriage, proceeding from faith and love to Christ and therefore of moral value — but not superior to the married state. The powerful impulse to marriage is resisted because of the prior claims of the kingdom of God. Such an internal renunciation "for the sake of the kingdom of heaven" is only a specific application of more general sayings regarding self-denial (cf. Matthew 16:24-26).

The first two classes mentioned by Jesus were familiar to his Jewish audience (cf. Yebamoth 8:4-6). All eunuchs whether from birth or emasculated by man were excluded from the assembly of the Lord (Deut. 23:1; but notice the prophetic word of Isaiah 56:3-5). The emphasis on marriage was strong in Judaism: "No man may abstain from keeping the law, *be fruitful and multiply,* unless he already has children" (Yebamoth 6:6). *Shammai* would be satisfied with two sons to fulfill the commandment and *Hillel* with one son and a daughter. The words of Jesus regarding the possibility of a single life transcended these views. To voluntarily renounce marriage for the kingdom of God, to concentrate all energies on goals

beyond natural factors, these were indeed revolutionary concepts. Christians should be free to enjoy or renounce all natural goods, including marriage. The
order of creation is affirmed by the Gospel, but can
be denied for the sake of the kingdom, because the
new order transcends the old one of creation. Jesus
and John the Baptist refrained from marriage for the
sake of the kingdom of God. Critical situations may
demand such renunciation and celibacy can be the
demand of the hour (I Corinthians 7:26ff). Marriage
can sometimes hinder an unconditional response to the
call of God (Luke 14:20). The positive statements of
Scripture regarding marriage from the very first page
of the Bible are so well known and universally accepted
that it is not necessary to mention them. But the
possible value of celibacy, especially for the sake of
the kingdom of God has received scant attention.

From the middle of the second century, celibacy
played a large role in the church. The rabbis had
taught unanimously that the duty of every Jew was
to have children. When Christians of Greek background became a strong element in the church, celibacy was lifted on a pedestal never intended by Jesus.
Already Justin Martyr speaks of many "both men and
women who have been Christ's disciples from child-
hood, who remained pure, (i.e. single) at the age of
sixty or seventy years." He boasts that he could produce
such from every race of man (Apology XV). Athena-
goras writes: "You would find many among us, both
men and women, growing old unmarried, in hope of
living in closer communion with God." (A Plea for
the Christian, XXXIII). Tertullian speaks of **John**

as "a noted voluntary celibate of Christ's." Virginity is celebrated by Cyprian who died in A.D. 258.

A misunderstanding of the saying of our Lord led to abuse and the Emperor Constantine was forced to legislate against the practice of self-mutilation. A canon of the assembly which met in A.D. 318, in Nice, Bithynia, dealt with the same problem. Celibacy, however, was encouraged, especially for the clergy. Bishops, presbyters and deacons were encouraged to have no further intercourse with their wives whom they had married while they were still laymen. At the council of Nice it was suggested that this should be enacted into a canon, but saner opinions prevailed. It was decided to leave the matter to the discretion of those involved. Those assembled were reminded of the ancient (!) tradition that those who were single when they entered the holy orders were required to remain unmarried. The subsequent development in the Roman church is well-known.

The situation remained fluid for awhile. The historian Socrates reported: If a clergyman in that country (Thessaly), after taking orders, should sleep with his wife, whom he had legally married before his ordination, he will be degraded. In the east, indeed, all clergymen, and even the bishops themselves, abstain from their wives: but this they do of their own accord, and not by the necessity of any law; for there have been among them many bishops who have had children by their lawful wives, during their episcopate.

Canon X of the council of Ancyra (A.D. 314) reads: "They who have been made deacons, declaring when they were ordained that they must marry, because they were unable to abide so, and were afterwards married, shall continue in their ministry, because it was conceded to them by the bishop. But if any were silent on this matter, undertaking at their ordination to abide as they were, and afterwards proceeded to marriage, these shall cease from their diaconate."

Canon XIX states: If any persons who profess virginity should disregard their profession, let them fulfill the term of digamists. And, moreover we prohibit women who are virgins from living with men as sisters. The punishment for digamy was, either one year of seclusion or one or two years suspension from communion. The word digamist is used for those who made a vow of virginity, (they betrothed themselves to God) but married later, contracting a "second marriage." A Canon of the council of Neocaesarea reads: If a presbyter marry, let him be removed from his order (i.e. from the exercise of the priesthood).

It is against this one-sided emphasis on the superior merits of the so-called angelic life that the reformers rightfully protested. They restored marriage to its rightful place. But the word of Christ remains valid. Some should remain single for the sake of the kingdom of God.

> "I want you to be free from anxieties. The unmarried man is anxious about the affairs of the Lord, how to please the Lord; but the married man is anxious about worldly affairs, how to please his wife, and his interests are divided. And the unmarried woman or girl is anxious about the affairs of the Lord, how to be holy in body and spirit; but the married woman is anxious about worldly affairs, how to please her husband. I say this for your own benefit, not to lay any restraint upon you, but to promote good order and to secure your undivided devotion to the Lord."
>
> I Corinthians 7:32-35

For centuries the missionary enterprise of the church has been carried out by single persons! The monastic orders played a significant role in the spread of the Gospel. The emergence of the Franciscan and other mendicant orders in the thirteenth century was associated with the growth of the cities. Their purpose was to bring the Gospel to the urban population. The great missionary advances into Central Asia and other remote areas were due to the untiring efforts of men and women associated with the monastic orders. For centuries the dissemination of the Gospel was the burden of single men and women.

In our day young people should be challenged to consider the possibility of a single life for the sake of the kingdom of God. (Such a decision may be temporary, in view of a specific task, here or abroad.) It is certainly not God's will for all single persons — but it it undoubtedly his design for some and each single person should honestly face this issue in the presence of God.

The scripture speaks of both deacons and deaconesses. Phoebe may be a case in point (Romans 16:1). It is somewhat difficult to determine whether Paul refers to a fixed office or simply to her services for the community. The official function is perhaps confirmed by the words of Paul to Timothy. The apostle defined the qualifications of the deacons and added: "Even so *must their* wives be..." (I Timothy 3:11 AV). The Revised Standard Version, says more cautiously: The women likewise.... The reference is probably *not* to the deacons' wives (AV) nor to women in general (RSV). The context speaks only of church officials and the four qualifications which follow (serious, no slanderers, temperate, faithful) correspond to the first four required of the deacons (serious, not double-tongued, not addicted to wine, not greedy). The absence of "their" (added in the AV) and the usage of "likewise" (RSV) which seems to mark a new ecclesiastical class, all point to deaconesses. This was the unanimous view of early expositors and is maintained by many modern exegetes. Phoebe was representative of this class. Deaconesses ministered to the poor, the sick and strangers. The order of deaconesses spread rapidly in the early church. Unfortunately much was added to the simple scriptural injunctions.

Deaconesses were not ordained but formally appointed. Often called "widows" and associated with them, their responsibility was to instruct new female converts and to assist with their baptism. Gradually perpetual virginity became a prime condition and a vow of chastity was imposed. Canon XV of the council of Chalcedon (A.D. 451) decreed: "A woman shall not receive the laying on of hands as a deaconess under forty years of age, then only after a searching examination. And if, after she has had hands laid on her and has continued for a time to minister, she shall despise the grace of God and give herself in marriage, she shall be anathematized and the man united to her."

Toward 1830 a new emphasis on deacons and deconesses originated in Germany. The first center for deacons came into being through the inspiration of pastor Johann Hinrich Wichern. Certain conditions had to be met to be accepted in the deacon-house. The single life was mandatory for those who aspired to become deacons. If and when they were appointed to a task, marriage became equally mandatory.

Centers for deaconesses are traced back to pastor Theodor Fliedner (1836). Applicants submitted to a one year trial period, followed by a noviciate lasting from two to six years, crowned by a formal dedication. Marriage was not allowed and when it occurred the position of deaconess was forfeited.

Regardless of the specific forms the order of deaconesses took in the early centuries of church history, regardless of subsequent abuses and disregarding the renaissance in Germany, the institution of deaconesses is scriptural and should be part of every church. The precise form may have to be determined by local needs since the biblical requirements are minimal (I Timothy 3:11; Romans 16:1, 2). Why not involve thousands of young persons as deacons and deaconesses to help new converts, children, the poor, the neglected, the underprivileged, etc.

A word about widows. Across the pages of God's word, special attention is focussed on widows. These teachings are neglected or ignored. But widows are not only the objects of special concern, they can also be involved in a practical ministry. (Read especially I Timothy 5:3-16). The age limit of sixty mentioned by Paul was soon disregarded. Gradually an order of widows came into being, following bishops, presbyters and deacons in importance. The modern application of Paul's admonition demands creative initiative under the guidance of God's spirit. Besides, the activities and organization of a church need not be limited to the New Testament pattern. Sunday schools are only one illustration of this truth.

In an age when many young persons are single, the local church should take some special action on their behalf. Some should be challenged to hear the words of Jesus anew regarding the single life; a new emphasis should be placed on the service of deacons, deaconesses and widows. The loneliness of older persons and their all too frequent plight (be they widowed or married) should also become the special concern of the church.

Sheer statistics will convince anyone that many persons who would like to be married will remain single. There are four widows to one widower! For this reason "lonely people have to be warned against themselves, for they may see as a possible solution to their problem only an immediate return to an earlier pattern of life. Widowers tend to seek a wife and widows a husband; but because there are four widows to one widower, and in our culture men generally suggest marriage, they remarry more quickly than do widows. This results in the women in the latter group fearing that they will not be able to find a husband; and when they are not in a group of prospects, they become panicky about their chances of escaping lasting loneliness. Some lonely people tell me that they evaluate every adult member of the opposite sex as a possible marriage partner, but many fail the imaginary test of eligibility."[1]

This attitude is not limited to widows. "In many spinsters the desire to marry becomes so intense and obsessive that they are robbed of their natural charm, ease, and spontaneity whenever they are in the presence of men. Their desire becomes thus their obstacle to marriage. They cannot look at a man, even one who has the least chance of ever marrying them, without thinking of that possibility. They are so troubled by this that the Christian surrender is the first condition they must meet if they are eventually to find a husband."[2] It is never easy to accept celibacy. Such surrender is only possible through divine grace. It is precisely this yielding to the will of the sovereign God which transforms a self-centered life into one of self-giving. Resentment and bitterness only increase isolation and intensify withdrawal. Self-preoccupation is not attractive.

"The self-giving woman, resolutely throwing herself into an inspired and outgoing vocation with the impulse of love that her heart needs to express, has found her home and spiritual family in the sick, the lonely, the poor, and the children whom she has met on her way. This has kept her in the reality of fellowship. This has saved her from sliding into selfishness."[3]

Marriage does not automatically guarantee happiness and fulfillment nor necessarily the end of loneliness. In the judgments of Theodore Bovet "the first point to grasp is that the overwhelming majority of these lonely people are in some way immature; they can neither set up nor maintain either the erotic tension of a love-relationship or the I-Thou tension of a friendship...as soon as they (the lonely) realise that they too can mean something to someone, and that their love is not despised, and as soon as they learn to face normal human tasks and responsibilities, they are saved."[4] The real issue is not celibacy or marriage, but the establishing of the right relationship with God which, in turn, will enable us to be correctly related men, loving, serving, responsible; in short yielded to God and dedicated to serve him among men. True, loneliness may be more acutely experienced by the single person, the burdens of married life are different — not necessarily lighter. The grace of God is sufficient for all the circumstances of life. Nothing can separate from the love which flows from God and therefore Christians can be more than conquerors and live triumphantly.

1. Southard, H. F.: *How Can I Learn To Live Alone and Like It,* Presbyterian Life, November 1, 1967, p. 4.
2. Tournier, Paul: *Escape from Loneliness,* Westminster Press, Philadelphia, 1962, p. 83.
3. Ibid, p. 85.
4. Bovet, Theodore: Op. cit., pp. 197-198.

11

THE BALANCE

He was driving down the road. It was a gray, dull day and suddenly he had a strange feeling of detachment, as if the whole world had become unreal. It was difficult to determine how long it lasted. The point was not duration, but intensity. The feeling was so pronounced that it eliminated all other sensations such as hunger and fatigue. Oncoming traffic jarred him back into reality. It was a momentary experience of loneliness.

——— · ———

She walked in, knocked off her shoes and fell into

a chair. It was an evening like any other. Listlessness invaded every member of her body. To get up and prepare supper for herself seemed pointless and uninspiring. The sense of frustration gained the upper hand. It was a momentary experience of loneliness.

—— - ——

Loneliness is often a mood and defies precise definition. It is an oppressive weight, a burden. The dominant color is blue. One feels abandoned, forsaken, lost. Silence becomes deafening. The radio is professional and distant. The D.J. tries hard — too hard; he cannot reach me. Music might stir the emotions but seldom heals the wounds. They have probably been inflicted by self-pity, but this knowledge only aggravates the situation. One feels guilty to be lonely, but the reality of loneliness persists. Perhaps it came suddenly. Someone left. The door closed and the room became a sepulchre, or a prison. To go out and mix with people does not really help. Television distracts for awhile, but then every remedy is temporary. For one thing, television has few redeeming values and besides, fun demands to be shared. It is hard to laugh, enjoy and learn alone. This is a fatal word — alone.

Thank God for the framework of existence. Life would be unbearable if it were not for certain compulsions. If it were not necessary to go to work and earn a living, or to keep house, one might be tempted to stay in bed — what then? The incentive may be a poor one, but necessity is real and because choice is impossible, the problem is solved...for a moment at least. I must, so I will get dressed, go to work and move through the day willy-nilly. Since the problem hasn't heally been solved, the evening is difficult, especially if no activity is planned. Loneliness is a plague, a disease, self-inflicted and seemingly as curable as selfishness.

Millions of people move through life day after day in gray monotony and utterly lonely.

Autarky?

This rare word describes a most desirable condition, one of self-sufficiency and independence. The old stoic philosophers used it to describe the self-reliant person, rich in inner resources. Paul does not hesitate to use this very word — *autarkeia* — to inform his readers that he has learned, regardless of circumstances, to be *content* (Philippians 4:11). External circumstances — Paul was in prison at the time — did not deeply affect him. He was independent, not of grace, but of surroundings. He had inner resources because he was in fellowship with God.

Elsewhere the admonition to be content, to be satisfied, is based on the fact that God has promised: I will never fail you nor forsake you (Hebrews 13:5). This is the cardinal experience. It had been voiced by Philip when he said to Jesus: Show us the Father and we will be satisfied (John 14:8). To know God as Father, as the one who cares, who is for us, who creates and redeems, this is indeed satisfaction, contentment. There is no other basis. Philip's request implies his belief that Christ could satisfy it. He did. "He who has seen me has seen the Father." The invisible God became visible in Jesus Christ. God now has a face. Jesus proclaimed God as the Father, the God of love and care. We have seen the Father — and we are satisfied. Things invisible and eternal are now seen in clear perspective. They have preeminence. There is a certain detachment

from external circumstances, a deep-seated satisfaction
and sufficiency. The basic problems are settled. Inner
strength flows from the new assurance of God's forgiveness. God's grace is sufficient, it is all we need.

This viewpoint does not lead to stoic indifference.
Detachment does not mean lack of involvement. It
does, however, mean that loneliness is largely conquered, that circumstances are no longer the determining factor. In fact, divine grace abounds so that we
have all sufficiency, blessing in abundance, not only for
our own needs, but more than enough for others also.

The assurance of divine forgiveness, the practice of
the presence of God, inner strength based on God's
grace, this is autarky, self-sufficiency in dependence
upon God. So it is indeed true that godliness with contentment is a great gain (I Timothy 6:6).

—— · ——

Man is a social being. He needs relatedness, fellowship. On the other hand, he is anxious to express his
individuality and uniqueness. One aspiration should
not be sacrificed at the expense of the other. Neither
should yield to the other. Man is held in dialectic
tension, a paradox to himself. It is difficult to achieve
a balance. As Emerson expressed it: Solitude is im-
practicable and society fatal. We must keep our head in
the one and our hands in the other. These conditions
are met if we keep our independence, yet do not lose
our sympathy.

Long ago, the proper balance was indicated by Jesus
Christ, when in answer to a question regarding the
most important commandment, he said: The first is
to love the Lord with all your heart, soul, mind and
strength. The second is to love your neighbor as your-

self. There is no other commandment greater than
these. To be a well-adjusted person certainly means no
less than normal mental and emotional development,
and balanced interaction with other people. This cannot be achieved without a secure basis, a foundation
which can only be found in God.

One of the most inspiring and dominating thoughts
in the words and works of Jesus was the truth that
God is our Father. He teaches, that as it is the very
nature of the Father to give good gifts to his children,
so it is the very nature of God to give his good things
to those who ask him. In fact, even upon those who
will not receive the best, he bestows much; he makes
his sun to rise on the evil and sends rain on the un-
just. What Jesus teaches of man's relationship to God
and vice versa is determined by this truth. On God's
side, there is love, acceptance, forgiveness. Positive response is expected from man, such as trust and love.
That God is for us, is indeed good news. That guilt
can be erased and forgiveness experienced really makes
a difference. Once this new relationship with God has
been established by faith in Christ — for he is the way
— the second commandment which is like unto the first
comes into its own. Balance is achieved between independence, a self-sufficiency resting on God's grace,
and inter-dependence, a relationship of love and service to others.

The right relationship with God does not automatically solve every problem. It could even be that
the amount of effort and energy expanded to overcome
loneliness is disproportionate to the immediate results.
Every learning process is difficult. He who tries chess
or tennis for the first time develops either a sore mind

or sore muscles. The acquisition of any skill demands
time and although basic thought patterns and character
traits may change under the influence of a new govern-
ing disposition, a desire to please God, maturity is not
achieved immediately. A gradual, progressive growth
is necessary.

But the fact that life has new meaning creates a
fundamental difference. It is no longer necessary to
cling to the dramatic role of the lonely one. Friendship
can now become a two-way street because we have
learned that it is more blessed to give than to receive.
There is little danger that Christian friendship would
deteriorate into a doctor-patient relationship. Even
the loneliness which comes from sudden deprivation
can be overcome. No longer do we live in a world of
make-believe. Delusions are swept aside. No longer do
we need to refuse all comfort in a vain effort to keep
the departed person present. Christians do grieve, but
not as those without hope. Once life is firmly rooted
in God a degree of autarky is achieved immediately.

The greatest search in life is no longer for a suitable mate as the main solution to the problem of
loneliness. Of course, to wish for such a relationship is
perfectly normal and healthy, but it is understood that
marriage per se is not a cure for loneliness and doomed
to fail as therapy. Involvement with other people is
no longer used as a crutch. It springs from a genuine
concern and becomes a rich experience of sharing
activity and creativity.

All the crutches mentioned previously, be it television or club membership, radio or group travel,
everything can now be enjoyed freely not to shut out

thoughts and escape from reality, but to stimulate thought and enjoy the present.

The man who has become a Christian has undergone a revolutionary experience. From here on in he has new values, a new outlook and therefore quite naturally new interests and a new interpretation of experiences. Neglected skills will be updated in order to serve our fellowman. A new realization sweeps over us that God has given us all things richly to enjoy. The outlook becomes positive because the good news has been heard and the inevitable result is joy in the presence of God.

12

CONCLUSION

When Henry James had attained fame and a secure financial position, he said to Somerset Maugham: I wander about these great empty streets of Boston and I never see a soul. I could not be more alone in the Sahara.

In a recent Reader's Digest article Billy Graham wrote: "I am often asked, 'What is the one problem that plagues more people these days than any other?' The questioners usually react with surprise when I answer in a single word: 'Loneliness.' "[1]

129

It is a great temptation to blame loneliness for absolutely everything which ails us. The single person assumes that a partnership in marriage would solve every problem. But the frustration which characterizes our generation regardless of age, marital status or socioeconomic level cannot be explained quite so simply. It is too easy to assume that everything would be different if only loneliness could be overcome. Loneliness is a tremendous factor, but it must be realized that in every crisis moment we stand alone — with God. In hours of decision we choose alone. No one else can or should decide for us. The decision to marry, the choice of vocation, the response to God and similar decisions remain our personal responsibility.

The loneliness of the leader and of godly men tests and matures character. Ultimately death must be faced alone. In some areas loneliness is unavoidable.

For the Christian, loneliness on the deepest level is cured. Man is reconciled to God and enjoys divine approbation. The Christian is at peace with God and conscious of God's love. The words of Jude are a powerful antidote against loneliness: Keep yourselves in the love of God (v. 21). Be aware of his love. It is the nature of love to give, to share. God so loved that he gave. It is the inevitable result. God gives regardless of response. His love is not conditioned by response. Christ died for the ungodly, the helpless, the sinners. God's love is his eternal self-communication regardless of response.

Since it is more blessed to give than to receive, God is indeed the blessed God. He is the great giver; he is never on the receiving end.

The Christian is not only conscious of God's care

and love but in turn controlled by the love of God, i.e., the love which originates in God and flows from God. This love now characterizes the believer. Self-centeredness yields to concern for others. Under the impulse of divine love the Christian gives himself... to others. He learns the secret of happiness because it is indeed more blessed to give than to receive. This love does not remain an idle feeling or a noble emotion. It becomes tangible and moves from compassion to involvement. Genuine Christian activity — not as a form of escapism but — motivated by divine love, a genuine giving of oneself breaks the grip of loneliness.

If the act of turning to God has delivered the believer from the most basic loneliness, the Christian life inspired and controlled by love cancels the loneliness between man and man. Christian activity is not necessarily or exclusively church related; but, motivated by the love which flows from God, it issues in a service of reconciliation and redemption. At this point loneliness is largely conquered. The temporary remedies and crutches advocated by superficial people for superficial problems can be discarded. The meaning of loneliness is discovered. It is a goad stimulating the search for God. The experience of loneliness points to God who alone can fill the void and give a new dimension to life. Reconciled to God through Jesus Christ by faith I am assured that God is for me and I can live triumphantly in the consciousness of God's love. The challenge of the Christian life is to radiate this love, to demonstrate it in life and death and through it to overcome loneliness on every level.

"So we know and believe the love that God has for us. God is love, and he who abides in love abides in

God, and God abides in him...there is no fear in love, but perfect love casts out fear."

1. *Loneliness: How it can be cured*: Reader's Digest, October, 1969, p. 135.